BLOOD LEGACY

A TRUE STORY OF
MURDER AND BETRAYAL

Judith Reitman

AN ONYX BOOK

ONYX
Published by the Penguin Group
Penguin Books USA Inc., 375 Hudson Street,
New York, New York 10014, U.S.A.
Penguin Books Ltd, 27 Wrights Lane,
London W8 5TZ, England
Penguin Books Australia Ltd, Ringwood,
Victoria, Australia
Penguin Books Canada Ltd, 10 Alcorn Avenue,
Toronto, Ontario, Canada M4V 3B2
Penguin Books (N.Z.) Ltd, 182–190 Wairau Road,
Auckland 10, New Zealand

Penguin Books Ltd, Registered Offices:
Harmondsworth, Middlesex, England

First published by Onyx, an imprint of Dutton Signet,
a division of Penguin Books USA Inc.

 REGISTERED TRADEMARK—MARCA REGISTRADA

Printed in the United States of America

Author's Note

Blood Legacy is a true story based on events surrounding a murder that occurred in Southampton, New York, in the spring of 1985. The names of some of the people mentioned in this story, marked with an asterisk, have been changed to protect their privacy.

They had the mental understanding of the shadings of right and wrong but none of them had the moral understanding of these things. They were the true, inborn criminals that can neither be changed nor modified.

—*The Bad Seed*

But she wasn't going to be poor all her life. She wasn't going to sit down and patiently wait for a miracle to help her. She was going to rush into life and wrest from it what she could.   —*Gone with the Wind*

Acknowledgments

Blood Legacy was a roller-coaster ride. The dips, twists, and turns in the story forced me to keep reassessing fact versus illusion, what the story appeared to be and what it truly was.

What remained constant was the encouragement and support from my family and friends. My father, as always, facilitated my being able to fully concentrate on this project without the more temporal distractions. My mother and sisters, particularly Laura, breathlessly awaited each new chapter. My attorney, Philip A. Byler, won my battle to keep this book intact.

I am particularly grateful to Belynda Sabloski, who allowed me to accompany her along her journey and entrusted me with painful recollections. Rosalind Campanella was forthcoming and uncensored. Kay Waldrop provided essential insights. The siblings of Arlene Caris gave me valuable perspective on Arlene's formative years. As for Arlene Caris, she spent many hours sharing her most intimate thoughts with me, and I wish to thank her for her tenacity and patience during much of this grueling process.

Special thanks to the detectives at Troop L who made this book an adventure: Don Delaney, Steve Oates, and commander Walter Heesch.

Michaela Hamilton saw the uniqueness of this story and guided me into deeper explorations. John Paine was my brilliant editor. And thank-yous to Jory Des Jardins, for her care and follow-through during the editorial process.

PART ONE

Chapter One

Belynda Sabloski watched her husband intently as he reached for the phone.

"It's Arlene," Fred said.

Belynda sat up in bed. "Is she okay?"

She had been expecting the call, hoping that her mother's initial bizarre reaction to her husband Bob's death had simply been a coping mechanism to deal with the sudden loss. Reality had hit a day later, Belynda thought, as Fred listened on the phone. For some reason, she felt a sense of relief. That Mom had acted so blasé wasn't right. Bob Caris deserved to be mourned.

Fred cupped his hand over the receiver. "She wants us to come over, right away. Roz and Tony are having a hell of a fight. Arlene's afraid Tony's going to kill Roz."

Fred assured his mother-in-law that they were

on their way. Fred Sabloski, for twenty years a shipping engineer at Grumman Aviation in Calverton on the east end of Long Island, was not one for histrionics. Hardworking and steady, Fred was the kind of man Bob Caris envisioned for his stepdaughter, Belynda. But by marrying Belynda, Fred had had to adjust to a world of emotional turmoil. The source of that angst was not his wife, who was a loving, levelheaded woman, but her family.

He could see from the start that they were a wacky bunch. But Belynda was warm and compassionate, and very sexy. He sensed that she had suffered in her first marriage, maybe as far back as childhood, but she disliked talking about the past. Fred was raising as his own Belynda's two daughters, Lori, sixteen, and Monica, eleven, and he and Belynda had had another child, Rebecca. The Sabloskis had a successful marriage, thanks in part to their remaining at the periphery of the Caris family dramas.

Now, at eight in the morning on their sleep-in Sunday, Fred and Belynda were hastily dressing. Admittedly, they had never gotten a call like this from Arlene. She sounded uncharacteristically desperate.

Fred glanced at his pretty blond wife as she pulled on a T-shirt. Her face was flushed with anger. "I know, honey," he said.

"Mom is more upset about Roz and Tony fighting than about her own husband dying," Belynda said. "Something's not right. And why hasn't she thrown that dirtbag Tony out already?"

Even as she spoke, Belynda knew she was asking a rhetorical question. Her stepsister Roz had always been Mom's favorite, and her every whim was granted, from clothes to cars to a career criminal husband. Roz and their brother Wade were Mom's "love children." They could do no wrong. Belynda had always been expected to clean up their mess.

Fred and Belynda made the drive from their house on Willis Avenue to the Caris residence in less than five minutes, through the sleepy streets of Southampton in its post–Labor Day recovery. During the summer Job's Lane was bumper-to-bumper with the Mercedeses and Jaguars of weekending New Yorkers and the flashy Porsches of the Hollywood crowd. America's bluebloods, the Rockefellers and the Fords who bought islets near the Caris home, sported beat-up station wagons or Hondas. By September each year, Southampton's enviable version of Palm Beach's Worth Avenue was virtually deserted.

Belynda rolled down her window and inhaled the salty ocean breeze. It already promised to be a warm day. It should have been a day for her own recovery. Bob's death had devastated Belynda. He had been in Saudi Arabia for nearly five months when he suffered his first heart attack. Mom said she had spoken with his doctor and he told her that Bob had recovered fully. But this second attack had killed him.

As Fred pulled up to the curb, Belynda spotted her mother in the driveway. Arlene was talking to Tony; she seemed calm. The thought again crossed Belynda's mind—Why hadn't Mom rushed to Bob's bedside when he first took ill? Why didn't she seem the least bit upset about his death?

Belynda squeezed her husband's hand and reluctantly got out of the car. Neither relished these rare visits. More than six months had passed since Fred had last set foot in the Caris home. That day he sat in the kitchen with Bob, drinking beer, as they talked in quiet voices, two peacemakers amid a cataclysm of women.

Tony turned to the couple as they walked up the driveway. An Italian bodybuilder with long, straight, dark hair and a temper to match his bulging muscles, Tony reminded Belynda of a monkey, the way his eyes were set so close together.

About seven months earlier, Rosalind had met her future husband on a blind date while he was serving time on assault and drug charges. Shortly after that, they were married in Denamora Prison in upstate New York. Released from his latest sentence in August, Tony had joined Arlene, Rosalind, and her five-year-old illegitimate daughter, Danielle, at 40 Adams Lane, a quiet residential street framed by manicured lawns and stately homes. At that time Bob still had not returned home from Saudi Arabia. Belynda surmised that he probably knew nothing about Roz's marriage; he certainly would never have agreed to Tony's moving in.

"Belynda, Fred," Tony said abruptly. "Good-bye."

With that peculiar announcement, he walked down Adams Lane, toward town.

"That lazy bum, I'm sick of him," Arlene said. She was dressed in slacks and one of her usual brightly colored polyester tunics. Belynda had dubbed her "the Polyester Queen." She saw that Arlene had gained considerable weight. Despite the heat, her fleshy white arms were covered with goose bumps.

As they followed Arlene through the back door, Belynda noticed the rosebush she had given Bob and her mother in June for their fourteenth wedding anniversary. It remained unplanted, still wrapped in its red ribbon.

When they walked into the kitchen, Belynda

was at once taken aback by its shocking condition. More than six months had elapsed since she, too, had been in her mother's house and now the once fastidiously neat Cape Cod was a pigsty. The stench inside was unbearable.

Rosalind was sulking by the television with her daughter. Belynda saw that her sister had gained weight—Roz had always been voluptuous, but her face was still lovely. Her blue-green eyes were puffy, as if she had been crying.

"Well, what was that all about?" Belynda asked her stepsister. "Tony sounded like 'Hail and Farewell.' "

"It is," Roz said. "He stayed out all night with one of his whores."

Belynda expected a stinging rejoinder from her mother. Arlene jumped at any cue to insult Tony. But she now was oddly quiet. Suddenly, as if an urgent thought crossed her mind, Arlene said, "I've got to find him." She hurried out the door.

"Why is Mom going after Tony?" Belynda asked. "I thought she wanted to get rid of him."

Rosalind shrugged.

"Roz," Belynda said, "let's go upstairs. I want to talk to you."

Driving to her mother's house, Belynda had resolved to get some answers about Bob's sudden illness and as sudden death. At the very least, she wanted the name of his attending physician in Saudi Arabia, where he had been consulting. For months, Arlene had been skirting the subject of Bob's heart attack. She said she had been in touch with his doctor via Bob's shortwave radio and that he had been receiving the best care. Still, why hadn't she gone to him? For five months Arlene had answered Belynda's questions perfunctorily, brushing off Bob's illness as if he had simply had a bad cold. Why had she kept changing the subject when Belynda asked for an address where she could write, a phone number? Something did not make sense.

As Belynda followed Rosalind to the second floor she noticed that the stairs were littered with dozens of air fresheners. As many deodorizing Stick Ups were plastered to the walls. The sickeningly sweet smell of Airwicks made Belynda want to retch. Roz had said there was a dead animal in the walls.

"For God's sake!" Belynda said. "Why doesn't Mom call in an exterminator?" The smell intensified at the landing. She held her hand to her nostrils and closed the door to Roz's bedroom.

In the living room, Fred settled into an armchair. Roz's daughter, Danielle, leaned against his leg. They were watching cartoons when, the next thing he knew, Belynda was flying down the stairs as if she had seen a ghost.

His wife grabbed his shoulders, screaming and crying. "Let's go! We gotta get out of here!"

"Honey, what is it?"

Belynda pointed to her sister, now standing in the hallway. "Tell him! Tell him what you told me!"

Fred's chest tightened. He felt fear like a knot twisting in his heart. "Will someone please tell me what the hell is going on?"

"Mom killed Bob." Belynda's face seemed to have aged ten years.

"I don't believe this!"

"It's true," Rosalind said. Her voice was flat. "He died six months ago. He's upstairs. In the attic."

"That smell!" Belynda shouted as she swept Danielle into her arms. This was no place for a child. She hurried toward the back door. "Call the police!"

Fred Sabloski was not going to call the cops for a dead raccoon in the attic, and he said so.

Rosalind looked drained but calm. And almost relieved. "Okay," she said. "I'll show you."

The call came into Suffolk Police, Riverhead Station, at nine-thirty. Investigator Donald Delaney picked up the phone. At thirty-six, Don Delaney was a third-generation Irish cop. His father had been a first-grade detective in New York

City, and his grandfather had been deputy chief inspector on the New York force. Raised in the Riverdale section of the Bronx, Delaney had served in Vietnam, then returned home to earn a degree in education at Manhattan College and wait for an opening at the police academy. His boyhood dream had been to become a cop. He graduated number two at the academy, first on the shooting range, and first in physical education.

Delaney married his high school sweetheart, Kathleen, and in 1973 began his career in law enforcement as a highway cop with the Parkway Police in Belmont, Long Island. He went on to earn a master's degree in human relations, a skill that came in handy when dealing with both victims and perpetrators. In 1985 he had been with the New York State Police for five years. A year later, he would be promoted to sergeant, then on to senior investigator, and, in 1987, supervisor of the New York State Police, Troop L, Major Case Squad.

Delaney was well liked and highly respected. He had a boyish charm and a perennial excitement about his job, about life. And he was tenacious. "I always get what I set out to get," he often said.

On the morning of September 8, he was filling out the usual damage charts from the previous night. Most of the calls into the station at the east end of Long Island concerned embezzlements, narcotics, rapes, armed robberies, and burglaries of the luxury boats that moored along Shinnecock Canal and the ocean. There were a few Chinese dump jobs, Chinatown gangland killings in which the bodies were dumped out east, and maybe one or two local murders a year. Nothing spectacular. There did remain an unsolved murder dating back to the early 1980s, a "gypsy-type" woman found dead in the sand dunes on the southern tip of Long island. She'd been nicknamed Montauk Mary.

The woman crying hysterically on the other end of the phone on this quiet Sunday morning said her mother had killed her stepfather, that he was in the upstairs hall closet. Within minutes Don Delaney was in his car, followed by troopers Mark Pouch and Frank Wakefield, speeding toward the Sabloski residence at 25 Willis Street, Southampton. Before he entered the Caris home he wanted to make sure there was sufficient cause to investigate.

By 10:20 a.m., Don Delaney and state troopers Pouch and Wakefield had learned enough from Fred and Belynda Sabloski to proceed to the Caris residence at 40 Adams Lane. Barely an hour had passed since Belynda had returned from her mother's home and called the station, but Delaney knew the pretty lady's life would never be the same. Her husband, too, was shaken, so shaken that Lori, their eldest daughter, offered to lead the police to her grandmother's house. Fred would ride beside her. As Lori got into her car, Delaney saw the little girl, Danielle, run outside.

"Aunt Lori!" Danielle called out. "Will you bring back my dolly?"

"Sure, honey," Lori replied. "Where's your doll?'

"In the next room to where Grandpa's stuffed."

Delaney suppressed a shudder.

Chapter Two

From the outside, the attractive saltbox with its impeccable lawn was indistinguishable from the other well-maintained homes on Adams Lane, one of the choicest sections of Southampton. The young woman who answered the door at number 40 had been expecting the police officers. Dark-haired and very pretty, with catlike eyes, Rosalind Campanella was sobbing lightly.

Delaney told Trooper Wakefield to remain downstairs and wait for Mrs. Caris, who had, her daughter Rosalind said, stepped out. Rosalind led the investigators up the stairs. Delaney counted at least thirty air fresheners, two per step, and he saw room deodorizers stuck on the walls. That only partly accounted for the smell in the house: acrid, pungent, sweet. It was the kind of smell you could not get out of your clothes or your skin. He had been a Marine in Vietnam. He knew the stench of decomposing flesh. But Jesus Christ, five months in this house? He heard Trooper Pouch's breath catch.

"It's here," Rosalind said. At the top step, she moved aside a trunk set in front of a low door that led to an attic crawl space. She reached in and began pulling out reams of tin-backed insulation foil—what appeared to be an entire roll jammed atop a mattress. The mattress, too, was rolled tight to fit inside the close space. It was stained with what looked like dark blood. The entire bundle was bound with heavy plastic.

Whatever or whoever that bulky form was, it had been literally cooking in that cumbersome "baggie" within the hot, confined nook. Anticipating the barrage of troopers and evidence investigators who would be called in, Delaney instructed Rosalind not to remove the body.

"I understand Mrs. Caris was responsible for killing him," Delaney said.

Rosalind replied, "Yes." She wiped tears from the corners of her eyes.

Delaney peered into the crawl space. The distinct smell of a body long dead mingled with the odor of mothballs and disinfectant. There must have been hundreds more air fresheners along the inner walls.

In the driveway a car door slammed. From the first floor Trooper Wakefield called out, "Mrs. Caris coming in."

Delaney hurried downstairs. Standing at the door was a bleached-blond matron, a panicked look on her face.

"What is going on here?" Arlene Caris's voice was shaky.

Delaney identified himself. "Mrs. Caris," he said. "We have reason to believe that there is a body in your house."

"Oh, my God! Oh, no! Oh, no!" Arlene clasped her hand to her chest and staggered. She looked as if she was going to have a heart attack.

Delaney had seen this reaction a thousand times: the heart begins pounding wildly, adrenaline shoots through the bloodstream. Mafia gambling busts routinely claimed they were having a heart attack, that they needed to get to a hospital, not jail. But this woman was clearly not faking. Delaney took her arm.

"It's all right, Mrs. Caris. Just relax." Gently, he led her into the living room, where she slid into an armchair. He sat nearby on a low ottoman, holding her hand, feeling as if he were calming his own grandmother. "Just relax. It's going to be okay."

Arlene looked accusingly at Rosalind, standing at the threshold of the room. "How did they find out?"

"I told Belynda," Rosalind said. She averted her eyes. "She was here with Fred."

Arlene's face flushed. Her hands trembled on her lap. Delaney motioned for Trooper Wakefield to take Rosalind into the kitchen. He wanted the story first from Arlene. Afterward, he would hear what her younger daughter had to say.

"There's just a breaking point," Arlene blurted out. "I couldn't take it anymore."

Delaney read Arlene her Miranda rights, explaining each one carefully. "Do you want an attorney present, Mrs. Caris?" he asked.

"I don't know, should I?"

Arlene was extremely distraught. She appeared to be much older than the late fifties he estimated as her age.

Delaney said it was her decision. Just then the phone rang. Arlene looked at the detective, who nodded his head to pick up.

Joan Brisset,* the Carises' neighbor, had seen the police cars. She knew from Arlene that Bob had died only the day before in Saudi Arabia. Was Arlene all right? Was there trouble? Could she help?

"He's dead," Arlene said flatly. "I lied to you. It was homicide. I'm responsible."

Delaney heard Arlene asked her neighbor whether she should call a lawyer. Brisset must have encouraged her to speak to the police. When Arlene hung up she seemed calmer, and waived her rights; she seemed eager to talk. It was clear to Delaney that she wanted to get this off her chest. He pulled out his notebook.

"Tell me what happened, Mrs. Caris."

"We were having an argument," Arlene began. "He, my husband, was harassing me. I'd been hurt, harassed by him. There is just a breaking point."

Delaney asked the date of the incident.

"March twenty-eighth," Arlene said. "But it lasted into the early morning, until three or four a.m. I wasn't sure of the time. Right after I shot him I heard a train whistle." Her chest heaved. "I couldn't take it anymore. He kept picking on me, pushing me around the bedroom. He said terrible things about me, my children. I had to put a stop to it."

"So there was an argument," Delaney repeated. If she had been defending herself against her husband's attack, she would have a good chance at a self-defense plea.

"It was a terrible argument," Arlene said. "I shot him with a Mossberg .22. It was in the bedroom closet."

Delaney moved in closer, still gently. He did not want to lose her now.

Arlene said something about "mental agony."

If the shooting had occurred during a struggle, what position had she been in?

"I don't remember. I was in a cloud. I don't remember pulling the trigger."

Delaney could see she was thinking hard.

"People thought he had a heart attack in Saudi," Arlene said.

Delaney asked her whether the Mossberg was loaded.

"I always had a loaded clip in the .22, but the chamber was empty. He was lying facedown when I shot him. It was through the back of the head."

Delaney knew that battered women often saw no way out. They were too scared and worn down to even contemplate leaving. Their goal was to simply stay alive. He recalled one woman who jumped out of a moving car as her husband was beating her. Delaney would never forget the terror on that woman's face and the horrifying minute details of her husband's abuse. Her words had poured out, as Arlene Caris's were doing now.

Still, the shot had been to the back of the head. A niggling sensation crept into his gut.

Delaney tore a sheet of paper from his notebook and handed Arlene a pen. "Show me what happened, Mrs. Caris. Where were you in the room? Just try to recall, from memory. Where were you when you shot him?"

Arlene looked blankly at the paper.

"You said there was a struggle, Mrs. Caris. Where was your husband?"

"I think he was on the bed."

"On the bed. Was he sleeping?"

"No," she said. "He was lying on the bed."

"Where were you standing in the room when you shot him? Ten feet from him? Five feet?"

"I don't know. Let me think." Arlene drew a loose diagram of the room—the bed, the dressers, the closet. She drew an X where she had been standing, at the foot of the bed.

"Was he asleep?" Delaney asked.

"No, he wasn't asleep."

"You said you chambered the gun. Did he hear it? Are you sure he wasn't asleep?"

"Well, he might have been asleep."

"You went into the closet and got the gun?"

Arlene nodded.

"You chambered a round. Was he asleep or was he awake?"

"Well, I guess he was asleep. I just couldn't take it anymore."

"What was it you couldn't take anymore, ma'am? Can you be more specific?"

"I just couldn't take it. There's a breaking point."

"And then what happened after you shot him?"

"Rosalind and I dragged him upstairs. We

moved the mattress and his body upstairs. I rolled him off the bed and onto the floor and wrapped him in the bedsheets and a large sheet of plastic. I took the mattress upstairs first." Arlene seemed exhausted.

Delaney asked who else knew about the incident.

"Only my daughter Rosalind. I was not aware until today at about eight-thirty that Tony, her husband, knew anything."

Delaney instructed Trooper Wakefield to bring in Rosalind Campanella. The entire interview with Arlene Caris had lasted five minutes.

"Anybody know about a homicide at Adams Lane?" Detective Fred Nordt looked at his partner, Russell Ditsler. Ditsler shook his head. "That's news to us," Nordt told the Suffolk County homicide officer on the line. It was eleven-fifteen a.m.

The address was familiar to the Brooklyn-born detective. In the twelve years Nordt had been with the Southampton police force, he had often answered domestic violence calls at the Caris residence. Domestic altercations were always the most dangerous. Occurring generally at night, family disputes required officers to act as referees amid a lot of screaming, crying, and, sometimes, weapons—everything from kitchen knives to rusted lead pipes. Everyone at the station knew that if the police were summoned to the Caris house, they would be facing a volatile situation. The cops would invariably get a hard time from Arlene Caris's son, Wade Kirby. The guy was either fighting with one of his girlfriends or the kids who hung around Trout Pond. Kirby would always resist arrest, and his mother would accuse the cops of giving her son a hard time. But Wade had not been around for years. These days he was back in prison for the long haul.

Nor was the call this morning about Tony Campanella, Wade's brother-in-law, who had recently been released from jail after serving time on assault charges. This call was about Arlene Caris. She was the chief suspect in the murder of her husband.

Although Robert Caris had been a longtime resident of Southampton, Nordt had never met him. He had heard that Caris was a mild-mannered man, a widower with money when he married his second wife, who'd had kids, Wade Kirby among them. Hard to figure how a guy like Caris had married into that. The wife, a good-looking blonde, knew what she was doing, all right.

By eleven-thirty, detectives Nordt and Ditsler were heading toward the Caris house. Adams Lane bordered the estate section, where the lawns resembled golf courses and some of the homes had indoor pools and bowling alleys. High hedges hid winding driveways leading into the fifteen-acre spreads of billionaire old money, like General Blackjack Pershing. Pershing had built his own opera house on his property; Bill Paley, the chairman of CBS, later bought that outbuilding as a summer mansion.

The newer money—Mafia, Greek tycoons, Hollywood—purchased waterfront "off-the-rack" mansions built on potato farms that had moved farther east. Some of these homes were castles, with turrets, paving stones imported from European landmarks, even wet bars flown in from London for that "old money" look. One waterfront estate had its own saltwater aquarium stocked with lobsters.

Nordt had worked as a bodyguard on his days off, for Hollywood producer Roy Radin, and he knew that many of the elegant houses harbored some not-so-nice secrets: wild sex weekends, black leather Nazi S&M routines, drugs. Radin was later found dead on the West Coast, an unsolved murder that some said had to do with satanic cults.

By the time Nordt pulled up to the Caris house, the area had already been cordoned off by uniformed police. He recognized officers of the Bureau of Criminal Investigation, the BCI. Word had come down that this was a New York

State case; the state troopers had been called and arrived first on the scene. An affable man in his late thirties, Nordt did not want to step on anyone's toes, but he managed to talk his way inside. He peered into the living room and saw one of the investigators, talking to Arlene Caris and her daughter. The women looked nervous, but neither one was crying.

In Her Own Words: Arlene Caris

I met Bob Caris in 1970. We had a mutual friend, Clifford Cox,* who worked for ITT with Bob. I was a member of the Suffolk chapter of Parents Without Partners. So was Clifford. He was a handsome man, but he wasn't bigger than a bar of soap after a week's wash. I could eat peanuts off his head. He was a very good conversationalist and an intelligent man, but I just couldn't see myself dating him.

I joined Parents Without Partners mainly because they had family activities I could take my children to, like trips to Sterling Forest, into the city for the Museum of Natural History, things like that. Interesting places families could go and spend time together.

Cliff told me, "You and Bob would hit it off." I asked him, "Why would we?" He said, "He lost his wife last year. He doesn't know what to do with himself. He's not comfortable not being married."

But I was getting a new business off the ground. I was working every moment I wasn't putting my head on the pillow. I told Cliff, "Give him my phone number. If he calls and I'm not there, tell him to leave his name and phone number. I'll get back to him." I told him to tell his friend I couldn't promise anything more than that.

Bob called several times before we were able to talk. Our schedules were clashing. The first date I had with him, I met him at Kate's,* my sister-in-law who lived in Islip. We arranged to meet there. I didn't know what to expect. That's why I didn't leave myself open to some private situation.

In 1970, I wasn't seeing anybody. I had broken up with Rosalind's dad, Robert E. Lotz, Senior. I married Bob Lotz on October 15, 1962. I split up from him in '66. I didn't have anybody in my life, really. Frank McDonald,* one of the men that was my partner in Five Star Trucking, I used to see him at the general meetings. I enjoyed talking to Frank. He was widowed. He had three young children. He was a good conversationalist.

At one time, I was engaged to him but once I accepted the proposal, he became so crude I called it off. I could work very successfully with him, but as far as my personal life was concerned, I told him it wasn't going to work. It would be like hitching two jackasses backwards. We became engaged in '69, but it didn't last very long.

Bob struck me as a perfect gentleman. I told him about my son Wade, his being charged with murder in Tennessee. I didn't pull any punches. When I told Bob what I was facing he seemed supportive of me. He stated he didn't know how he would handle something like that. I told him there's only one way to handle this: He's got to have a decent attorney.

Bob had an adoptive daughter, ever since she was a toddler. She didn't even know she was adopted until she was an adult. She certainly didn't show proper consideration for a parent that had provided a good education and all the comforts of life. He was hostile about it, he was hurt. Her letters were few and far in between. Phone calls, maybe twice a year, was a lot. It was a very strained relationship. I met her once before we were married.

My house was always open to them, my kids. They came and went. They knew where each other was going. They knew what my agenda was, if I was going to be away for a little bit. They knew where I was, how to get in touch with me, when I was coming back. This is the way I brought my children up. When I met Bob, I thought he was a caring, compassionate person. He was attentive to my needs. I was going through a heck of a rough time. He showed a lot of admiration for what I did, how I managed to maintain the schedule I did. I was working with Five Star. I had Wade and Roz to take care of. I had that legal situation with Wade to contend with. And then Belynda had her domestic problems.

Bob told me the thing that attracted him was my independence, my standing on my own two feet, facing and dealing with the lot that was handed to me. That was the case in my other two marriages. The very thing they claimed to admire in me was the very thing they tried to destroy. The old male ego. I felt I must be wearing a neon sign across my back that said, "Abuse me."

If I had the feeling this was too good to be true, I would have stopped it dead in its tracks and started looking, like I did with Bob Lotz. In dating Bob [Caris] there was no red lights. It seemed very normal. He struck me as being almost shy. He turned a hobby into a well-paying job. I had a considerable income myself. I knew the money was there. I was not looking at his salary. I was looking at him as a person.

He started with his nonsense within three to four months after we were married. The best part of my life, my children, were loyal to me. Bob didn't have that, he never had. Sharon (his daughter by his first marriage) is a greedy little grubber. Give me, take, snatch, however she can get, that's exactly what she is. Daddy held the purse string. He made good, darn good, money.

The first incident was when I confronted him about his trying to alienate Rosalind and me. When he was taking my jewelry and putting it in her jewelry box, and putting her jewelry in mine, I said, You know, every week she did not bring this stuff down and make the switch. She doesn't have to. All she has to do is tell me she would like to wear something of mine and I don't ask her to put hers down here in exchange. Never have and don't intend to. This is as obvious as the nose on your face, that you are trying to create trouble between mother and daughter. And it won't work, so just knock it off right now.

With that he hauled off and slapped me. He started calling me everything but a child of God: a bitch, a slut, a whore. When he slapped me, I threw water in his face. I was angry. I was hurt, and yet I didn't have the desire to strike him. I figured if I threw water it would put a stop to it and he'd have to take care of his discomfort and he'd leave me alone, which is exactly what it was, the same as with Bob Lotz and Tommy Kirby, both of them. And to me it was a repeat, the third time, a repeat of violence. He knew he was wrong. Instead of apologizing for what he did, he went out and bought a beautiful card, a special card. In the card he put, I think, fifty dollars in it.

But you know, it had no meaning for me. I was disillusioned. How in God had I made another mistake?

I didn't tell her [Belynda]. I didn't tell anybody. I didn't even tell Roz. She was quite young. At that particular time, I don't think he had touched her and he was trying to convince her what a nice guy he was, how good he could be with her, what he could do for her, and what he could buy for her. But there was something nagging about that. Why was he trying to turn a daughter against her mother? Wouldn't it be a much happier relationship, the three of us, where she thought as much of him as a youngster could think of a father, a stepfather? But he was not her dad and I tried to instill in her that he was her father. She was old enough to know he was not her father.

That's the way their relationship started, in trying to alienate her affections from me. He was the good guy, Mama's the bad guy. It didn't work but it upset Roz. It upset her very much. And everything went downhill from there. It was within the first year, I'd say within the first six months. I didn't see it coming and I didn't believe he was capable of it. I had confidence in him. And I didn't want to believe that anything like that could happen with him. I didn't want a repeat of any part of the two previous marriages.

There were a number of times I tried to tell Belynda and let her know things were not as they seemed. One time, she was over there when he had come in, and he had a beautiful card, a special card, For Someone Special. He must have paid at least three dollars for it back then. Inside the card there was a hundred dollars, a hundred-dollar bill for me. When he put the card on the table at my place [it was] his way of apologizing but he'd never come out and say he was sorry. It was after the bout where he'd used his hands. Belynda said, Well, aren't you going to open your card?

I said, Well, it's quite easy for me not to be excited. It doesn't mean what it seems, what it appears to you to mean. This is conscience money.

That's exactly what it was. She just looked at me funny.

I tried telling her some time after this little incident. Every time I started to talk to her, tell her. . . .

Did you ever talk to somebody and they weren't listening to anything you are saying? It was like they had closed an invisible door in your face. That was the very same, the very feeling she gave me. And so I stopped. I didn't bother anymore. I don't think she wanted to hear, didn't want to hear that there was anything at all in my life that made me upset or unhappy. As far as she was concerned, I had no problems. I had a beautiful home. I had a good income, didn't have any money worries. I had it made.

Chapter Three

The last time Senior Investigator Theodore Niksa sprinkled Mennen After Shave on his face mask was when he found a body in the Taconic River. The victim, bloated and putrid, had been waterbound for over a week. But this, the stench at 40 Adams Lane, was much worse.

A big, soft-spoken man raised in Riverhead, Ted Niksa had been a state trooper since 1968. In the mid-seventies he was assigned to the narcotics unit in New York City for a six-month period, then transferred to the Federal Narcotics Task Force, the first such task force conceived. It was a two-hour commute every day from the east end of Long Island, where he lived, to Manhattan, but the job was a challenge he could not pass up. The country boy soon won the respect of his city peers by his sheer audacity. In 1977, Niksa was promoted to captain and returned to the Riverhead state police, at that time headquartered in Islip Terrace. He handled all felonies in Suffolk County.

Arlene Caris and her daughter were, without a doubt, an odd lot. "If it were just a crime of passion you'd think it would've been done and reported, but here she stashed the body for months and months," Niksa told his commanding officer, Lieutenant Walter Heesch. The men were standing on the front lawn, which had been cordoned off with bright yellow tape. Reporters with TV crews, as well as neighbors, were already straining the line.

Niksa and Heesch were imposing men: one, a hefty Pole, and the other, a more austere Anglican. The immaculately dressed Heesch stood an impressive six-eight.

"If I had to design a boss to my liking," Niksa often said, "it would be Walter Heesch. He's very straight. You know where he's coming from. The job's first."

The body stashing was peculiar indeed, Heesch agreed. Serial killers generally secreted bodies or body parts as trophies—like Jeffrey Dahmer, who hid portions of his victims as a kind of sentimental, sexual perversion. But there was something very strange about the Caris case. True, when people kill they act irrationally, and when they dispose of the body they also act irrationally: dump it quick on the side of the road, freeze it and run it through a compactor or wood chipper, toss it into a fast-moving river. But keep it in your own house for months? How could anybody have lived with the stench? Heesch wondered. Even from where he stood, the smell of decomposition was overpowering. Could the occupants of 40 Adams Lane simply have gotten used to that smell?

Heesch and Niksa entered through the front door. After a cursory glance into the living room, where Delaney was interviewing Rosalind Campanella, they proceeded up the stairs, taking care not to disturb the dozens of air fresheners before the evidence clerk had made his tally.

Another member of Troop L was on his way from his home in East Quogue. Brisk, handsome, with bright-blue eyes, Steve Oates had intended to spend a quiet Labor Day with his wife and young son. But he was on call as Delaney's backup for weekend duty, and made the twenty-minute drive in ten. When Oates pulled up to the Caris house, Lieutenant Heesch took him aside and briefed him. It looked to Oates like a package case. They had a body, an ID, and a crime scene. They had a defendant and she was under arrest. The worst part, having to tell the relatives that their loved one was dead, was, at least, not a factor in this case.

When Heesch informed him of the location of

the dead man, Oates rolled his eyes. Whoever heard of somebody committing a murder and stashing the body in the attic? Except of course in movies. Unbelievable.

Oates familiarized himself with the layout of the house, following the scattered path of Airwicks and Stick Ups. There were dozens in every room, in nearly every square foot of the house. Their density increased on the second floor, where there was a sparsely furnished bedroom. The notion of someone sleeping in that room appalled Oates. To him, the place smelled like the worst garbage dump in the dead of August.

Oates positioned himself at the top of the stairs by a small open window and awaited Dr. Johnathan Arden's arrival. The investigator had great respect for the county's medical pathologist. Several years earlier, they had worked together on the homicide investigation of Darwish Ali Darwish, the Palestinian stabbed to death and dumped on Heckshire State Parkway. Arden really knew his business, even if it was, in Oates's estimation, a very peculiar one.

As the medical examiner's van pulled up, Oates wondered how they were going to get the body outside without everybody losing their breakfast.

Soon Arden came into the house. Seemingly unfazed, he crawled into the attic for a cursory check of the body. "You're not going to open that thing inside, are you?" Oates asked Harold Fay, the medical examiner's photographer.

"What do you want to do?" Fay replied.

"Take a look at what's downstairs." Oates pointed at the secluded backyard, where a picket fence enclosed a small shed. The yard was neither visible nor accessible from the front of the house. Given the extraordinary circumstances, they decided to unwrap the body outside.

At 3:20, the bulky form, still contained in its cocoon of bedding material, foil-backed insulation, all bound in a Simmons Maxipedic mattress, was carefully withdrawn from the attic. By 3:45, the mummified package was out the door. Ten minutes later, the body of Robert Caris was unwrapped. Arden observed that the body was remarkably well preserved.

"How you guys doing down there?" Oates called from the upstairs window.

Fred Nordt's partner Russ Ditsler, looked up at him. Oates saw that his face was pallid.

"What's that on Caris's wrist?" Oates called out. "A watch?"

Ditsler said it was a Timex.

"See if it's still ticking."

"No, it's not. It says 3:50."

Oates looked at his own watch. Caris's Timex

was right on the mark. The man had taken a lickin', but his Timex kept on tickin'.

Even before Don Delaney saw the autopsy report or learned that Robert Caris had been a rather frail-looking man, he knew in his gut that he had a tight case for cold-blooded murder. He believed Mrs. Caris's pose as a victim of abuse was a ruse. He had interviewed battered women. He had heard the terror in their voices as they described the beatings in great detail. Some were even afraid to leave their own house for fear of their husband's reprisals. But Arlene seemed different.

What bothered Delaney most was her inability to answer questions about the alleged abuse. She could not come up with specifics. What exactly had her husband done to torture her? What couldn't she take anymore? Delaney figured that at some point in time Mrs. Caris had decided to get rid of her husband. But why keep the body in the house? She could have easily disposed of him and removed herself, at least physically, from the crime scene.

Delaney also wondered about Rosalind's part in this scenario. Had she stumbled unwittingly onto the scene, or had she been an accomplice? For reasons he did not yet know, Arlene Caris had wanted Bob Caris permanently out of the way, and her daughter had been willing to comply.

Don Delaney barely recognized the woman who walked into his office at five o'clock. Belynda Sabloski appeared to be sleepwalking as her husband, Fred, escorted her gently to the detective's desk. The preliminary information Delaney had obtained from the Sabloskis earlier that morning had been sufficient for him to believe that a crime had, indeed, occurred at 40 Adams Lane. Eight hours later, he had a confession, and the accused in Riverhead jail on a charge of second-degree murder, the highest count in New York. Rosalind had been booked on first-degree hindering prosecution, then released. She had agreed to turn state's evidence.

Delaney also had an impressive evidence tally that included a .22-caliber Mossberg rifle used to shoot Robert Caris, a Ruger Model 10-22 carbine, one spent shell casing taken from the Mossberg, and five unexpended rounds of ammunition and one ammunition clip from the Mossberg. The Ruger had one clip and a Scope Mount in a leather case. The lady clearly liked guns. The troopers had also confiscated a considerable number of prescription medications, including tranquilizers, painkillers, sleeping pills, and diet pills.

Belynda and Fred each recounted the events

leading to the call to Delaney; their statements were typed and signed.

"Mrs. Sabloski, do you know who 'Sundance' is?" Delaney asked as Belynda stood up to leave.

She said she had no idea.

"Do you know who Wade Kirby is?"

"Of course. He's my brother."

"Do you know where he is?"

As far as she knew, Wade was working as a culinary chef in New Orleans. At least that's what her mother had told her. Wade was an outstanding Cajun cook. Belynda believed that her younger brother, who had a long criminal history, had finally turned his life around.

"Your brother is in prison, Mrs. Sabloski," Delaney told her. "He is serving fifteen years to life for rape."

By Monday morning, reports of the Caris murder were making lurid media headline. The *New York Post* bannered its story: "After man's rotting body is found, cops charge: Granny Guns Down Gramps and Stuffs Him in a Closet:"

A 56-year-old grandmother was jailed on murder charges after authorities said she settled a spat with her husband by shooting him in the head and hiding his body in a closet for five months. . . . In a signed statement Mrs. Caris told state troopers that she killed her 68-year-old husband, Robert, "to put a stop to the bickering and hostility. He was continuously picking on me and pushing me around," she said. . . . At one point her husband pushed her off the bed. . . . "I took my Mossberg .22 caliber rifle from the bedroom closet with the intention of shooting him and putting an end to it. He was lying on his stomach on the bed when I fired one bullet into the back of his head."

Mrs. Rosalind Campanella, the paper reported, told investigators she helped her mother carry the body upstairs to a closet. "I tied a rope around his chest and pulled him up the stairs while my mother was lifting from below. . . . We put him in the storage closet and my mother put a roll of insulation on top of him. We closed the door and put a trunk in front of it."

"They apparently ignored the smell," Investigator Donald Delaney was quoted as saying.

That same morning, Suffolk County Medical Examiner Dr. Johnathan Arden conducted the autopsy of Robert Caris. The body was in a severe state of decomposition, but the path the fatal bullet had taken was unobstructed by decay.

The bullet entered the left occipital area (the left side of the rear of the head) and followed a path extending forward and to the right at approximately a forty-five-degree angle, and slightly upward. It had perforated the brain, depositing a trail of tiny metallic fragments. The track of the missile ended in the right frontal area (the right side of the front of the head), where a severely deformed, small-caliber bullet was recovered.

There was no doubt as to the distance from which the shot was fired. Arden observed black, burned gunshot residue on the skull and its lining membrane that surrounded the entrance wound. This, along with the skull fractures radiating from the entrance wound, indicated that the muzzle of the gun had been touching Caris's head when the shot was fired. He had been killed by a single gunshot wound, at close range, while he was lying facedown. Most likely, he had been asleep.

At two-thirty that afternoon, Tony Campanella strode into Don Delaney's office, prepared to tell what he knew about the murder of Bob Caris. By then Delaney knew he would be interviewing a violent, mentally unstable individual.

Judging from the computer rap sheet on Gerard Antonio Campanella, Rosalind's husband had had a hard time staying out of jail. He had been so rarely "on the outside" that his marriage to Rosalind had taken place in prison.

At twenty-four, Campanella had spent most of his adult life either locked up or awaiting sentencing. To his further discredit, Arlene's son-in-law liked to fight cops.

Campanella was Brooklyn-born, but his first arrest, in 1978, at age sixteen, had been for felony possession of stolen property in Suffolk County, where his family had moved; the charges were dismissed. In March 1979, he was again arrested for possession of stolen property. While awaiting sentencing, he was arrested in January 1980 for burglary; in March, again for burglary; in April, for resisting arrest, disorderly conduct, and burglary third degree; in May, for driving while intoxicated and again for resisting arrest; in June, for burglary; and in August, for third-degree escape, resisting arrest, and criminal mischief.

Delaney was struck by the unusual dismissal of drunk driving charges. But what concerned him more at this point in Campanella's criminal history was his obvious disregard for authority. Few people resisted arrest. Delaney later explained, "Most people willingly go with you when you arrest them. They let you put handcuffs on them, because, first of all, they know you have a gun. You are the police department, and they have all sorts of ideas about what could happen if they ran. Resisting arrest usually means you are dealing with an assaultive, violent personality."

Campanella copped a plea to the earlier criminal mischief charges and was sentenced in December 1980 for a maximum of one year. While imprisoned, Tony still managed to get into trouble. A charge for possession of contraband and selling it to prisoners added sixty days to his sentence.

Shortly after his release, Campanella was rearrested in March 1982 for unauthorized use of a vehicle—a charge that was dismissed. In May of that year, he chalked up his first arrest for assault with attempt to cause physical injury.

The assault charge was dropped, Delaney noted, because of Campanella's "incapacity due to mental disease or defect." Campanella had been judged to be mentally deficient. Yet that dismissal did not occur until January 1984. While still out on the streets, presumably in a state of mental imbalance, he was arrested in July 1982 for criminal mischief, and in August for selling drugs.

Delaney took issue with the court's determination of mental defect and how it handled such cases. Too often courts subjected the public to risk. "When a person is a true schizophrenic and does not know the difference between right and wrong, he should not be handled the same way as someone who intentionally commits a crime. Society needs to be protected from people who have mental disease. They should be locked up in mental institutions. However, the laws release these people when they have supposedly gained their sanity."

"Transient schizophrenia" appeared to be Tony Campanella's ticket to freedom.

By the summer of 1983, Campanella had expanded his forays into Connecticut. His first out-of-state arrest occurred in Norwich; the charge was burglary and larceny. At that time Tony was calling himself "John Baxter." That year he was also arrested as a fugitive from justice. In June 1984, Campanella was sentenced to serve time in the "big house," as Delaney called the state prison facilities, for two to four years. A little over a year later, he was released, and he moved into 40 Adams Lane where his new wife, her daughter and mother were living with a body in the attic.

Campanella appeared to be very nervous. He was on parole until October 1987 and told Delaney he did not want to jeopardize his parole. Sure, he had known about the murder, knew the body was up in the attic. But what would this mean to his parole?

There was no law requiring an individual with knowledge of a crime to report it to the police. But Campanella's ignorance of that fact gave Delaney some leverage. Delaney needed his cooperation, and so he intended to handle Arlene's son-in-law with kid gloves. He was going to be Tony's buddy. Delaney assured him that as long as he had had nothing to do with Caris's murder and would cooperate, he was not going to get into trouble.

Campanella seemed eager to talk. He told Delaney that in early April 1985, while he was an inmate at Clinton County Correctional Facility, he had phoned his wife, Rosalind. She had told him her mother, Arlene, had killed Bob Caris.

Had she given any details? Delaney asked.

"Roz said she didn't hear the gun go off. It was early in the morning, and Roz and Danielle, that's her daughter, they were sleeping."

What else did she say?

"She said her mother woke her up, crying. My wife went downstairs and she saw Bob Caris. He was lying dead on the bed."

In her statement to Delaney the day before, Rosalind had said she had told no one of the murder. Now Delaney learned that her husband had known about the crime a week after it occurred. Rosalind was, Delaney figured, just trying to protect her incarcerated husband.

But there was another discrepancy. Rosalind had told Delaney she heard arguing that night, but closed the bedroom door and went to sleep. That morning she said she found her mother downstairs, crying; yet she told Tony that her mother had awakened her.

"So Caris was lying dead on the bed," Delaney prompted.

"Yeah. I asked her where Bob was and she told me he was up in the attic. I thought, 'Holy shit.'"

Several days later, Campanella said, he'd received a letter from Rosalind. "She wrote me her mother said she 'got rid of the problem,' which was her husband."

Where was this letter? Delaney asked.

"It's at home."

Delaney contained his excitement as Campanella continued. "I got another letter from her, also talking about how her mother had got rid of her 'problem.'"

"So you knew Caris was in the house."

Campanella squirmed. "Yeah. But hell, man, I never even knew Bob Caris. Roz said he didn't know nothin' about us getting married."

Arlene had told him the smell was dead squirrels and raccoons under the roofing. "She must've thought I was pretty dumb," he said.

Sometime in early September, Campanella

overheard Rosalind and Arlene talking about their "little secret upstairs in the storage space." After Arlene went to work, Roz took him into the attic.

Delaney found it curious that Roz had not shown her husband the body immediately upon his arrival in August, but he let Campanella go on.

"So this smell was really bad. I saw a mattress and fiberglass insulation inside. I told my wife the next day that we got to get the hell out of here. Because of the body inside and the smell."

Still, Campanella had known since April that Bob Caris was in the attic, dead. Why the sudden decision to move? "Had you said anything to Arlene about finding the body?" Delaney asked.

"No, not till later. She drove me to the station yesterday, and she said she shot her husband."

Did she say why?

"No," Campanella said.

At Campanella's departure Delaney reviewed the statements he had thus far taken. He was intrigued not only by the murder and the secreting of the body in the attic but also by Arlene and her two daughters. Even under duress, the mother appeared to be a contentious force. Her daughters were quite different from each other, in both personality and appearance and their relationship with their mother. While the younger,

Rosalind, was willing to accommodate Arlene in the murder of Bob Caris, Belynda had turned her mother in. Whatever her internal battles, Arlene's older daughter had been able to make a difficult and painful emotional and moral decision. Belynda did what was right.

Delaney speculated that in the course of this investigation he was going to learn about a very unusual, if not highly dysfunctional, family—a family that, he believed, pivoted around a woman who had murdered her husband in cold blood and lived with his remains for nearly six months.

In Her Own Words: Arlene Caris

I always like to see the best in my children, in all things. Then something materializes that you are not happy about. You never thought your daughter would do such a thing. Well, there it is, right before your eyes. There's no denying it.

When I first learned Belynda was pregnant with Lori, I didn't think my daughter would conduct herself in that manner. I gave her credit for having stronger morals, higher moral principles. It hurt. Since then, things have happened. She knew she was wrong. I never suggested she terminate the pregnancy. I asked what her feelings were. She was not a thirteen-year-old kid. So she wanted her baby.

Belynda was my firstborn, my darling little girl, a beautiful child that I loved and adored with all my heart. My sons were just as adorable. I loved them just as much. But there's something special about your firstborn. Kirby, the father of the three older ones, I was in love with him. I wouldn't have stayed with him and put up with the crap I did for eleven years if I didn't care as much for him as I did.

I didn't have the baby right away. I was married at 18. I was almost 21 when Belynda was born. It wasn't that I tried not to have any children. It was circumstances. I could not have them. I had three pregnancies that aborted naturally. When I asked my doctor why, it was because I had a cyst in my ovaries. I just couldn't carry them further than that.

I had the cysts removed. In the waiting period that had been prescribed, I got pregnant with her and carried her to term.

I had a toxic pregnancy with her, hit me the first month. It was no joke. I often told her it was a wonder her face didn't look like a toilet bowl—that's where I was most of the time.

She was the first. There is only fourteen and a half months between her and Joel. I had a good pregnancy with him. He was a good baby. A good child.

Belynda was twelve and already starting to show some of her nastiness, deceitfulness. Telling me she was going here when she'd be there, that sort of thing. It got to where a character, a hot item with the police, was concerned, was sniffing around her, bringing her little trinkets. She was a kid. He was twenty-one, twenty-two, twenty-three years old. I put a stop to that nonsense. I told her I didn't like it, it's something not right here. I told his mother, "I don't want your son paying attention, coming around calling for my daughter. This girl is jail bait. She's only thirteen years old. She is too young to date. I have not given her permission to date and certainly not a young man the age of your son."

I thought we were close. It was with hindsight, she had already been talking to this one, that one, anybody that would listen to her. Oh, her mother is this, her mother is that, what a horrible life she had, what a terrible mother I was. It was to draw attention to herself. After Rosalind came along, she didn't get the attention she thought she should. She acted like she thought Rosalind was the greatest thing she ever saw. I found out a number of years later that it wasn't true. She felt jealous, very, very resentful. What can you do in the situation like that? You have to make the best of whatever you can. Because she certainly wasn't neglected. I was there for her when she needed me. I was there when she was pregnant with Lori. And I was there for her when she left Dubin* [her first husband] and came to New York.

Belynda met Bob before we were married. He was not all that much of a person for showing enthusiasm or anything. He was a little stand-offish when he first met people. He was more or less a good listener. We were there when Monica [Belynda's second child] was born. As a matter of fact, Bob had driven the car to take her to the hospital when she went into labor.

I never told him about Lori's illegitimate birth. I can't put my finger on why, but just something (inside me) said "Don't." If I had, it would have been that much more ammunition for him.

Belynda thought Bob liked her because I never told her all the unkind things he said about her. Any and everything he possibly could. We were married in June. We hadn't been married six weeks when she and both the kids came up from Florida or Louisiana where they were living at the time. She left Dubin. The man was irresponsible. He wouldn't provide for his wife and family. He thought nothing of calling and asking me to send money for her. She came up here, bag and baggage, left him and with the idea that she was going to come at our expense.

Bob greeted her with open arms. But with me it's, "How the hell long is she going to be here? How long am I going to have to put up with her and them two brats?" She didn't know that. He was wearing two hats. A white one to her and a black one to me.

I wanted to talk to Belynda about what I was going through, let her know it was not all sunshine and roses. Belynda thought I had it made. Money, financial, creature comforts. I was constantly being abused, verbally and psychologically. More verbal, psychological. He was always demeaning and demoralizing me. I could not do anything to please him. He complained about everything, no matter what I did, I should have done something else. He was constantly belittling, demeaning, cursing my children.

He was trying to turn Rosalind against me. Roz had her little chores: she had to make her bed and she had to put soiled laundry in the laundry bag. When she came home from school she had to change her clothes. She was not to leave the house without my knowledge or consent. She had a nice big yard to play in, and she was expected to stay in it. I didn't allow her to roam the neighborhood.

When I left instructions for her, he [Bob] told

her she didn't have to do it. And he'd tell me she wouldn't do it to create problems. It got so finally I said, "This cannot be. This is a nightmare and it has to stop." Rosalind was no longer the happy little child that she was. She acted like she had the weight of the world on her shoulders. He wanted her to feel he was the good guy and I was the bad guy.

There've been times I was hurt physically. One of the shocking things was when I was awakened out of a sound sleep with a fist right between my eyes. It was before 1985. I confronted him as to what the heck is going on here.

"Why," he said, "it was an accident."

I said, "Accident, my foot. How do you accidentally punch somebody in their sleep right between their eyes?"

Oh, he vowed up and down that it was accidental, that he had flailed his arms out in his sleep and didn't mean to. But then not more than two or three months later, he did it again, 1983 or somewhere around there. It was after Danielle [Rosalind's first child] was born [in 1980]. This was after he had tried using the car as a weapon. He had attempted to drive the car head-on into a tractor trailer. It happened in 1981.

I had Danielle in the car seat. The first time it happened we were out to King Kullen [supermarket] in Bridgehampton to do our regular grocery shopping, and all of a sudden, I saw him whip that steering wheel right in the line, the path, of an oncoming tractor trailer. It was on Montauk Highway, the main street from Southampton East. And when I saw him do that I immediately kicked his foot off the accelerator and grabbed the steering wheel and whipped it as sharp as I possibly could to the right off the road.

I said, "What in the name of heaven are you trying to do! What are you trying to do, deliberately kill us, or is it just me you want to kill? Me and this baby?" He said he didn't have anything to live for.

I said, "For heaven's sake, you don't have anything to live for. You got everything in the world to live for. We got a nice home. We don't owe a lot of bills. We got income sufficient to take care of any and everything we could want."

I know in one respect why was he depressed and that was because he did not hear from his adopted daughter, Sharon. He didn't hear from her the way he liked to. She rarely picked up the phone to talk to him and as far as writing to him, the letters were few and far between. She thought that she was very badly treated because she didn't have the allowance a lot of the other kids had, but they were from families with more money. I can't talk for her. I don't know what her feelings were. She didn't choose to confide in me. As far as she was concerned I was a pseudo-mother, and yet one that she really didn't care that much about anyway.

How often did she write? Not often, very few and far between. When they did arrive, he didn't even want to open them. I had seen him leave her letters right on the table for days and days at a time.

He didn't have the rapport with her that I had with my children. He resented it, there was an awful lot of resentment there. I got the brunt of it because I was there.

I didn't leave because I was ashamed I had made a third mistake in my choice of a mate. I risked an awful lot because I was ashamed and I didn't want anyone to know the hell I was going through. That's how ashamed I was. The only one I talked to was Rosalind. I made several attempts to talk to Belynda about it, but she just slammed a mental invisible door between us. I just quit trying to talk to her. She didn't want to know.

Chapter Four

Arlene Caris professed to abhor violence. She would later explain, "I don't like violence. I never like to hear people argue. When people start to use argumentative tones of voice, I like to get away from it as quickly as possible. I don't like physical violence of any kind. I never did. I like to put distance between me and it."

Her eldest daughter would be very surprised at those comments. One time in her life Belynda had had to fire a gun and kill. Shooting her little beagle, Missy, had been a conscious act, something she knew she had to do. Otherwise what had been an accident, backing up her car and running Missy over, would have been a crime. A crime of suffering. She couldn't bury Missy, though. She was nineteen years old, had just had a baby, yet she had to wait for her father to come home, and bury her dog. She had lived with the memory of Missy's agonizing screams for years, and the sound of the gunshot that put an end to her suffering.

Not her mother. Mom used to stand out on the porch and shoot the dogs and cats that came into their yard. Shoot them like she was running an errand, taking care of business. Then she would dump their bodies in the trash bin. That's where, years later, Rosalind had found her own dog, Brandy, the one Danielle so loved. Mom had blown Brandy's head off and left her in the garbage bin. Mom had killed Brandy on Roz's twenty-first birthday.

But to shoot her own husband, the man she professed to love? The man who had given her everything? This is *my mother*, Belynda kept telling herself as tears poured from her eyes. My mother could not have done such a thing.

Belynda knew how hard it was to leave a marriage. She had finally left Paul Dubin,* but only after years of abuse. The trigger had been his hurling a glass at her that ended instead splitting open their baby's lip. Belynda told her two daughters that nothing bad was ever going to happen to them again. On the drive from Louisiana back to New York, Belynda had miscarried. That unborn child would have been her and Paul's second together. She stopped at a gas station, expelled a rush of blood and what looked like fecal matter, then got back in the car and kept on driving.

Still, she had not killed Paul. What could Bob Caris have possibly done to deserve death? Why couldn't her mother have just left him?

Shortly after discovering her stepfather's body, Belynda had called her favorite cousin, Kay Waldrop, in Georgia. Kay did not seem a bit surprised. "We half expected to hear she'd killed somebody," Kay said in her soothing southern drawl. "But we thought if she'd kill anybody it would have been you, honey."

What's more, Kay said, Belynda should not feel guilty for calling the police. "She's never been a mother to you, Belynda. You don't owe her nothing."

As Kay listened to her cousin weeping, she thought about Belynda's childhood, how she had tried to win Arlene's love. But to Arlene, children had simply been a necessary evil. The parenting Belynda had so desperately sought she had found, unexpectedly, in Bob Caris. Bob was the only real father Belynda had ever had. Even after marrying Fred, Bob remained Belynda's confidant, a thoughtful, kind man to whom she could turn for advice and warmth. Bob helped Belynda, not for gain but for love, the love a parent feels for a child.

"Belynda," Kay said, "she's never done nothing

but hurt you. You've got a husband, three kids you owe. There's nothing you can do for Arlene now. Nothing."

Kay knew Arlene was capable of anything. All those stories about Bob's heart attack in Saudi Arabia, her keeping up those lies while Bob lay dead in the attic. Only one thing would have surprised Kay: Arlene telling the truth.

"Belynda, she would have killed you in a heartbeat, and Fred, and anyone else if that's what it took to cover up what she did. She's crazy."

"Mom's crazy," Belynda said through her tears. "Crazy like a fox."

Kay's heart ached for her cousin. In one day Belynda had lost her father and her mother, one by death, the other by deception. What concerned Kay now was Belynda's future. She was going to have to look over her shoulder for the rest of her life. Because if there was one thing Kay knew for sure it was that Arlene would get even with Belynda for turning her in.

Dr. Jane Marion,* the Caris family's physician, had no doubt that Arlene Caris had killed her husband, most likely in cold blood.

Earlier on the morning of September 9, Belynda Sabloski had called Marion's office. Belynda's voice was muffled, riddled with pain. Dr.

Marion agreed to prescribe a mild sedative for her longtime patient.

As she awaited Belynda's arrival, Dr. Marion thought about the nature of self-determination. What enabled one child to escape a family's pathology? How had Belynda managed to grow and move on? Would she have the strength to face the terrible truth about her mother? Did Arlene even know she had done something wrong in killing her husband?

By what she discerned from her brief conversation with Belynda, Arlene had displaced responsibility for murdering her husband onto her eldest daughter. In the convoluted thought process so typical of a psychopath, Arlene Caris had shifted blame for her heinous act onto the person who turned her in to the police. Conveniently this was Belynda. Marion was not surprised at such transference.

Marion knew that the analytical processes of people like Arlene did not make sense. "You don't get from A to B ever," she later explained. "There are real detours. In Arlene's mind she had decided, 'The reason I killed my husband was because Belynda told the police.' That was how she would rationalize it. Sociopaths, or psychopaths, never think they're to blame."

Over the years Marion had seen the relationship between mother and daughter deteriorate, despite Belynda's efforts. It had taken a great deal for the young woman to overcome the kind of hardships she had endured, but Belynda had managed to put her life back together. She was no longer dependant on her mother, no longer under the influence of a woman who needed to exert absolute control over her children.

Belynda had worked very hard at being okay. And now Arlene had thrust a cataclysmic weight of guilt onto the only child who had managed to escape the family's pathology.

With the morning's headlines glaring back at her, Dr. Marion vividly recalled Arlene's glibness, her familiarity with a range of subjects, which made her an interesting enough conversationalist. But, more important, Arlene Caris listened very well. She could read people and focus her distorted lens on their vulnerabilities. But she had easily passed as a charming Southern woman in Southampton society, which placed a premium on "genteel" appearances. Arlene must have dazzled a sheltered man like Robert Caris.

Driving to Dr. Marion's office, Belynda felt as if she were sleepwalking under water; each movement of her limbs encountered heavy resistance. It was painful to keep her eyes open. There must be some other explanation for Bob's death, she decided. Something she could hold on to, to keep her sanity.

Maybe it had been Rosalind. Rosalind had killed Dad. That was it. Mom was really covering for Roz.

When Belynda returned home with Dr. Marion's prescription for a sedative, Fred told her the phones had been ringing constantly: reporters, friends, neighbors. But there were only two calls of consequence to Belynda. One was from Don Delaney at state police headquarters; the other, from her mother at the Suffolk County jail in Riverhead. She wanted to see Belynda.

Belynda called her aunt Kate Porter* and asked her to accompany her to the jail. Aunt Kate could handle it. She was a scrapper from Pittsburgh. Kate wouldn't take crap from anybody. She could stand up to Arlene.

Kate had married into the Porter family through Arlene's brother, the family's handsome son, Johnny Luke.* Aunt Kate had not lived with Johnny since their kids were little, but to loyal Kate, he was and always would be her husband. No matter who he had run off with.

As she drove to Kate's Islip home, Belynda replayed in her mind the morning's conversation with Don Delaney. She liked him, trusted him. For all the years she had tried to tell people about her mother, here, finally, was someone

71

who needed no convincing. Delaney saw Arlene Caris for who she really was.

This morning he had a peculiar request. "If your mother asks you to do something for her, will you let me know?"

Belynda wondered what her mother could possibly want of her now?

Three thousand miles away, as Belynda headed toward Kate Porter's house, Sharon Wheeler sifted quickly through the mail. Incredible. Six months had passed and still no word from her father. His letters had stopped around Christmas, a month after her husband, James,* had left their marriage for a younger woman.

For twenty-five years the Wheelers had had a picture-perfect life: three handsome, healthy sons, a lovely home in Northern California, lucrative careers, wonderful friends. James was an executive with a large corporation, and they had more than enough money. Sharon had everything she had ever expected from life.

Then, suddenly, everything fell apart. Now, when she needed her father most, he had uncharacteristically deserted her. At least, that's how it felt.

The first week of September had been particularly trying for Sharon. She was vice principal of a middle school and was expected to manage the usual glitches that come with the beginning of the school year. She felt woefully inadequate. After all, hadn't she failed to manage her own life?

Arlene's words of comfort, written earlier that year, had been well meaning but hollow—they were not from Dad. "God doesn't give us anything we can't handle," her stepmother wrote in mid-January. "We are better people for having faced these problems. There will be some 'good' come out of this situation somewhere down the road of life."

Arlene sympathized with Sharon's plight. What with Sharon's mounting bills and children who, despite their intelligence and sophistication, could not comprehend why their father had abandoned them. "I know what it's like to be abandoned," Arlene had written, "because it happened to me. I just wanted you to know I do know what a heartbreaking experience it really is."

Arlene had also written that Dad was not feeling well: a circulatory problem, "not too serious. I'm trying to encourage him to give up smoking, or at least cut down on it. I don't nag him about it for fear it will cause him to smoke more." Arlene always ended upbeat, requesting photos of Sharon's boys. "I wanted you and your family to be included as part of mine, when I married your Dad. I tried to make it so."

Still, Sharon sensed something was wrong with her father. For nearly forty years, ever since she was six, she could count on lengthy, weekly letters from her dad. For years those letters had been postmarked from Saudi Arabia. Over the years, her father's letters had changed little. They were rather prosaic, often ten typed pages, nothing particularly noteworthy. Dad was so low-key, his life so predictable. He was just keeping in touch, letting her know that she was still his "little girl." Every Friday, the same old boring letter.

But sometime after October of last year, those letters began changing, subtly at first. Dad's thoughts seemed disconnected, then progressively more rambling. Was he becoming senile? Or worse, had he developed Alzheimer's disease? Perhaps that was why Arlene had taken to writing and signing his name to those letters.

"I'm getting my old life back," Bob Caris wrote when he decided in 1971 to marry Arlene Kirby Lotz, two years after Sharon's mother had died. His "old life"—a family of three, a wife and a little girl.

Arlene looked surprisingly like Sally Caris. She seemed to make him happy. He was especially pleased about her young daughter. He even introduced Rosalind as "my little girl."

But for months now, whenever Sharon phoned, Arlene told her, "Oh, he just left . . . you just missed him. He still hasn't written you? I keep reminding him to write you."

The silence hurt terribly. And there was that gnawing anxiety that something terrible had happened to her father, something Arlene did not want her to know.

As she entered the Suffolk County jail in Riverhead at three-thirty, Belynda was immediately struck by the smell of urine. She and Kate signed in, were checked through metal detectors and then led down the reeking hallways. They progressed from one set of security gates to another, walking deeper into the belly of the prison. The bars closed and locked behind them.

The last enclosure opened into a visiting area. There were coffee shop–type booths and hard, molded-plastic chairs welded together. Belynda and Kate slid into a booth and waited.

As from some far-off place, Belynda heard security gates rattle open and slam shut. Somehow, within the last thirty-six hours, she had been catapulted into a foreign territory where there were no familiar signposts. There was only a palpable terror. But then, terror had a measure of familiarity; it had been her childhood companion.

Growing up, Belynda had been able to gauge her mother's mood simply by the way she walked into the house after work. It was not a game, this hurried assessment; it was a matter of survival.

Now her mother was walking toward her as if she had simply returned from a tiring day at work. Her expression was pensive, her movements unhurried. She's going to be nice to me, Belynda thought. She's going to be nice to me because she needs me to do something for her.

Driving to Riverhead, Belynda had told herself that she would let her mother explain. She intended to keep still. But when she saw Arlene she blurted out, almost hopefully, "Mom, did Roz do this? Are you covering up for her? Are you taking the blame for Roz?"

Arlene calmly looked from her daughter to her sister-in-law, Kate. "No, Roz did not do this," she replied. She enunciated her words carefully. Her Park Avenue voice, Belynda called it. "Belynda," Arlene said, "I want you to go to my house. In the kitchen cabinet there's a bottle that has Prince Romanov's name on it. I want you to get it."

Prince Romanov had been one of Arlene's private-duty patients when she worked as a home nursing aide. Romanov had died of cancer, a painful death that required strong sedation.

"Nobody will understand if they find that bottle in my house," Arlene continued, "so I want you to take it out of my house and I want you to throw it in the sewer in the middle of town. I don't want you to dump it in my garbage can or in yours. I want you to get it out of my house and take it to the middle of town and dump it."

They sat there for another twenty minutes, maybe more, but Belynda barely heard anything else her mother said. She did not know what was in the bottle. But she knew, right then and there, that Mom had killed Bob Caris in a calculated, planned execution. And now she, Belynda, was expected to risk everything to help cover up the crime.

"Suddenly a light came on and there was no more darkness," Belynda would later recall. "I knew in the depths of my soul what kind of monster my mother was."

PART TWO

PART TWO

Chapter Five

Arlene Caris's life began in Rossville, Georgia, along what the Cherokee called the Trail of Tears. Few epithets would more appropriately describe the tortured route along which the Southern Indian tribes were herded to Oklahoma in the 1830s. It was a prisoner march born of greed, deceit, and betrayal, ending in destitution and death.

The first steps along the Trail of Tears were taken in the summer of 1838 at Ross's Landing, the Tennessee border town named for Chief John Ross, patriarch of the Cherokee people. Ten years earlier, the Georgia legislature had passed an act that sounded the death knell for the Cherokee. Gold had been discovered on Indian lands, and it became imperative to remove its lawful claimants.

During those years, large areas of the Cherokee Nation were incorporated into the Georgia territory, tribal laws were nullified, and the Cherokee became subject to the white man's dictate. When the tribes refused to yield, an order was issued for their removal, and one of the most dramatic and tragic chapters in American history began.

Oppression was used to break the spirit of the Cherokee in Georgia and their Choctaw, Chickasaw, Seminole, and Creek compatriots across the southern states. They were plied with liquor, charged with debts, threatened, cajoled, bribed into relinquishing their native soil. When they resisted they were wrenched from their Smoky Mountain villages and forcibly herded westward. Men, women, and children were shipped over the Tennessee River in log flotillas and keelboats, packed like cattle in oxcarts lumbering across the drought-ridden, then frozen terrain of Kentucky, Missouri, and Arkansas, marched naked and barefoot through the worst drought the South had known, then on into rain and snowstorms. Entire villages were wiped out by fever, influenza, and starvation. In frontier towns like Nashville, Memphis, Marion, Springfield, and Little Rock, babies were pried from the arms of their dead mothers. The feeble drowned in the Hiwassee and Mississippi Rivers. Those who tried to escape were impaled on bayonets.

Generations after the last Indian footfall, despair still clung to the tinderbox towns along the Trail of Tears. There the descendants of Indian captors littered the Smoky Mountains with their shacks, trailers, and moonshine stills. The KKK imprinted its flaming signature where bark huts had once stood.

In the summer of 1927, a young Tennessean named James Clard Porter came to Rossville, Georgia, to seek his fortune. He was freewheeling and handsome, full of ginger and spice. Clard, as he was known, hailed from Spring City, Tennessee, which neighbored the town of Dayton. It was in Dayton where the Scopes "Monkey Trial" of 1925 expunged Darwin's theory of evolution. The Porters of Spring City had once been well off. Local lore had Clard Porter's father, John, winning half of Spring City in a gambling match. But at his death, his wife, Louella, who had been thirteen when she married the thirty-three-year-old Porter, was left with debts and nine children, fourteen-year-old Clard among them.

That summer of 1927, Queen Esther Johnston and her brothers earned some money picking peaches at a neighbor's orchard. Like the Porters, the Johnstons had once been a gentrified family. Before the Civil War they had owned plantations and slaves. By the early 1920s, however, they were struggling to raise peanuts and cotton on the hard, red Georgia clay.

Clard Porter would tell his children that the moment he laid eyes on Queen Esther (who was known as Esther), he knew she was going to be his bride. Esther was as smitten by the handsome Tennessean with curly dark hair and a reckless good nature. But in Ora Johnston's eyes, her future son-in-law was "poor trash."

Despite her mother's objections, Esther married James Clard Porter on January 29, 1928, her twenty-first birthday. Almost like clockwork, on November 16 Myrtle Arlene (who was known as Myrtle) was born in the border town where the Trail of Tears had begun. That day the headlines of the *Walker County Messenger* reported gains in cotton crops, the defeat of the high school football team, and a plea for peace at an Armistice Day service at which "Miss Edna Spencer very sweetly sang 'Keep the Home Fires Burning.'" Residents awaited with anticipation the total eclipse of the moon on November 27.

One year later, the country was plunged into the great collapse of 1929. Unemployment, strikes, and the threat of violence tore the nation apart. The Porters urged what produce they could from the red clay and produced a passel of children: Alice, Clara, Willie May, and brothers, Johnny Luke, and Heartsell. The family lived like sharecroppers on Missionary Ridge, once a look-out point during the Civil War. Clard worked as foreman of the peach orchard in exchange for a run-down farmhouse. He hired local men as pickers and at the height of the season recruited migrant workers.

Clard Porter was a rugged man. He played hard and worked hard. Until he changed his ways and became the deacon of the Baptist church, he was a real hell-raiser. Good-looking and gregarious, he made friends easily and retained their loyalty.

Clard, it seemed, also rode with the Klan. As Arlene's sister, Clara, put it, "The Klan was against white men who mistreated their wives or didn't support their children. Daddy'd make sure those men kept their butts up straight."

Theirs was a mountaineer existence. The Porters' ramshackle home had no electricity. When the well ran dry, the children hauled water from a nearby stream. Esther boiled the family's laundry in a cast-iron wash pot, and Clard built a double-seater outhouse to accommodate the growing family; discarded Sears catalogs served as toilet paper.

But despite the lean times, the Porter family never went hungry. Every fall Clard butchered his own cows for market, and whatever parts went unsold made their way to the Porter dinner table. Arlene's brother, Johnny Luke, would later describe one of those days on Missionary Ridge: "I remember that goat hanging up on the cherry tree and Daddy's pouring hot water through him to clean him out. A lot of people don't know how to kill goat, but Daddy could dress 'em and you wouldn't know it was goat. He'd hang 'em up by the hind legs, cut his throat and let 'em bleed. Poured hot water through 'em, then cold water. Keeps the hair off the fat."

In the tradition of Southern matriarchy, Esther Porter managed the family's domestic life. An excellent cook, she could disguise the more rangy game her husband caught.

Coon was, the children agreed, the best meat you'd ever want to put in your mouth. After Daddy'd catch possum, he'd cage it, and Mother would give it vegetables for a couple of weeks to clean out its system. Squirrel was also one of Esther's specialties. As Clara would later recall, "Mother would fry up the whole squirrel in the pan and as it got hot its head cracked open and then the brains seeped out. With the head there'd be a lot of meat, especially on the cheeks. Ain't nothing better than squirrel." There'd be plenty of biscuits and gravy at each meal.

Esther tended to the chickens and eggs, brought corn to the gristmill, churned her own butter, and rendered animal fat into lard and crackling—fried pork fat, which the children fa-vored. As talented a seamstress, she sewed all the family's clothes from flour and cow-feed sacks.

But for all her domestic skills, Esther Porter remained an aloof presence, the quintessential "iron butterfly," the kind of woman only the South can claim. She cared more about the man in her life than her children.

"Mean, spiteful, harsh," Arlene's sister Willie May would remember. "She could cut you in two with her eyes or her words."

Whether from frustration at their poverty or early memories of her own emotionally barren childhood, Esther Porter lashed out with rage, particularly at her daughters. The girls would have to fetch their own switches, and if the hickory was green and broke easily, Esther beat them double. She always drew blood. Clara would re-call, "Mother told us she wished she never heard tell of a kid."

The childhood that Myrtle Arlene recalls cen-tered around housework: changing and washing diapers, doing dishes, scrubbing floors, feeding the animals. She did not have friends, and even in school she remained aloof. The one person to whom she could turn for some measure of af-fection was her father. Clard was a jack-of-all-trades and a grand storyteller. His eldest daughter followed close at his heels, shadowing him in his chores. Myrtle listened with rapt attention to his stories about growing up poor in Tennessee, everybody raised to do for themselves, so many sleeping in the bed on a cold night. They had to pull together to survive.

She was drawn to that self-sufficiency and to the man who took on heroic proportions in her life. Her mother was jealous of that closeness. "Anything Mother could do to cause me more aggravation, any kind of humiliation. Anger, spankings, whippings I called them. Mother was not hesitant to rile her husband against the children." Clard Porter, too, had a temper and his wife knew his trigger points. But he held himself back from beating his children. More often he clenched his hands into fists and shoved them deep into his pockets.

One time, though, he did not.

The evening before Arlene's junior high school graduation, Esther agreed to let her borrow a dressy pair of shoes. Later that night, she accused her daughter of "sneaking" them out of her closet.

"You going to let that girl get away with that?" Esther asked her husband.

Clard Porter had had a rough day. When Arlene saw her father whip off his belt, she plowed into him, knocked him over the dining room table, through the kitchen and backward over the footboard of her parents' bed, which then collapsed. Then she tossed his belt into the furnace.

"I am tired," Arlene told him. "I am very tired of being punished for something I didn't do. I'm tired of having falsehoods told on me."

From then on she guarded herself with a wall of silence. She did not talk to her parents for the next two years, but she was never whipped again.

Her siblings recalled nothing of that episode or their eldest sister's self-imposed silence. Daddy never raised a hand to that girl, Clara and Willie May both said.

"Myrtle could never tell the truth about nothing," Clara later explained. "Like the marriages she said Mother arranged, said Mother picked out the sons of her friends and told Myrtle she was going to marry them, like it or not. And Myrtle saying she got to the altar four times, four times before she was fourteen! Each time saying no right to the preachers' face. That never happened neither. But Myrtle never could tell the truth about nothing. Mean, selfish, self-centered, scheming, she was. Making up fancy words she thought no one knew, just to make them all look like dumb hillbillies.

"Lie like a dog, Myrtle did."

Willie May also remembered those tall tales. "Oh, that's just Myrtle talking big, reaching for the moon," Willie May thought then. "But no sense in telling Mother about her tales or we'd all get beat for what she said or done."

Perhaps to shield herself from their family's hardships and her own loneliness, Myrtle Arlene created a grandiose internal life. Certainly there was little glamour in the heart of the Bible Belt. The Rossville Arlene knew as a child was a cow-town whose streetcars gave right-of-way to cattle drives. Horse-drawn wagons raised up dust storms on Main Street, where residents set out cardboard boxes to hawk whiskey and gamble. The Lone Star Saloon on the Tennessee side of the town line served the best hamburgers in town, but the sign outside read Men Only. Peer-less Drugs and Grocery Store boasted a basket-ball court on the second floor, and Gabby Hayes General Store charged everyone for a straw broom, whether you wanted one or not. The main event of the year was the Watermelon Cut-ting, rivaled only in the mid-1930s by an on-slaught of Gypsy caravans fortelling love and doom for the residents of Rossville.

The town was deeply divided along economic lines. Few felt that segregation more acutely than Myrtle Arlene. She would gaze longingly at the display windows of the Personality Shop and the JoAnn Shop, stores frequented by rich women. The good life seemed a million miles away.

In 1938, *Gone with the Wind* returned to the South its antebellum grandeur and romance. Ten-year-old Arlene decided she was not, after all, a Porter from Rossville. She told her sisters she had been switched at birth.

"What do you mean, switched at birth?" Clara was only five then, but the notion did not sit right with her. "How they switched you, Myrtle? You was born at home like we all was."

Myrtle Arlene insisted they had given Mother and Daddy the wrong baby.

"They, who?" Willie May piped up.

"My real mother and daddy's a rich family," Myrtle said.

"That where you learned them big words, acting like we're stupid and don't know what you're talking about?" Clara hated when her sister put on airs, always trying to be someone she wasn't. "That why you can't set down and just talk in plain English, Myrtle?"

Arlene told them that she had a younger brother whom she had never met. A real brother who was living the way she was supposed to, in a fine, big house with servants, up North. That's where she was going someday.

But that was Myrtle, reaching for the moon.

When Arlene was in her teens, Clard abandoned farming and was hired by Peerless Cotton Mills in town. Esther took a job at a local thread manufacturing company. As Clara saw it, "Mother suddenly treated Myrtle like a princess. She bought her better clothes, stopped the whippings. Things got good for Myrtle but for no one else."

When she was thirteen, Arlene cleaned houses after school. Her good looks gave her entry, a year later, into Miller Department Store in Chattanooga, where she ran the concession stand and waitressed at the in-store restaurant. Her goal was to be able to take care of herself. She did not want to be dependent on anyone. She wanted her freedom.

Then she fell in love.

Chapter Six

Arlene couldn't have chosen a better mate than Tommy Lee Kirby to make her mother's blood boil.

Before the Kirbys moved to Rossville, they had eked out a meager existence in the rocky hill country of Sparta, Tennessee. The extended family lived in clusters of mountain shacks with neither running water nor electricity. Generations farmed and worked the coal mines, often dying in underground accidents, or of "black lung." Talk in Rossville had Kirby Senior shot dead by his father-in-law for brutally beating young Tommy. The boy had accidentally stepped on a chicken running near the house and killed it, thus angering his father.

Kirby's widow, Maude, moved to Rossville. There she met her second husband, Max Rogers,* who worked at the Peerless Cotton Mills. Rogers was an alcoholic, and Maude—well, everybody knew Tommy's mother was a whore. "She'd lay up with anybody for a bottle of whiskey," as Willie May heard tell.

Arlene and Tommy first met when they were nine years old, as neighbors up on Missionary Ridge. They saw each other in school, but Esther discouraged any fraternizing with the Kirbys. In her opinion, they were a bunch of ne'er-do-wells.

Sometime during 1943, Myrtle Arlene again encountered Tommy Lee in Rossville while he was on leave from the Navy, where he was making his career. By then, she said, she had graduated Rossville High School, enrolled at the University of Tennessee, gotten her pilot's license, and was working a night shift at Southern Bell Telephone and Telegraph.

About all that's true is Arlene having worked for the phone company, said her sisters. Even then, she was working a day shift. Years later, when Clara retrieved her sister's high school records, the files showed that Arlene had attended only one year and that she still owed for unpaid lunches.

What her siblings knew for certain was that, for Myrtle, Tommy Lee fit the bill. He was fine-looking—a fair-haired Robert Taylor look-alike— and he was stationed with the Navy in Bremerton, Washington, thousands of miles from Rossville, Georgia. Tommy Lee was Myrtle Arlene's ticket out.

She arranged a transfer with the phone company to Washington, and in early August 1946, at age eighteen, Arlene flew to Seattle and a new life. On August 17, she and Tommy Kirby were married. Neither her family nor his attended the small ceremony officiated by a Navy chaplain.

Arlene wasn't interested in marrying a millionaire. She simply wanted a home, a husband, a family of her own. Not much to ask for.

Arlene soon realized she had less of a partnership than she expected. While Tommy was on duty, she was left alone for long periods of time. She accepted his erratic work shifts, but when he was assigned to sea duty off the China coast, he was gone for six months; they had only been married a year. Her telephone company job occupied her daytime hours, but she had no social life. Tommy's friends viewed her as a backwoods hick and talked down to her. Inwardly she smiled. They knew nothing of her resolve. When she made up her mind to do something, she was single-minded. She would clear the decks of whatever was in her way.

The decks turned out to be more crowded than she had anticipated. "Tommy thought he was God's gift to women," Arlene later recalled. "He was a good-looking character, but it wasn't never his fault, to hear him tell it. Women just fell all over him. True, some did. But he was after anything that rustled a skirt."

When Tommy was on leave, he had the use of his wife's car, a convertible. She had no qualms as long as he picked her up after her shift. But she soon found telltale signs in the car: cigarette butts, not Tommy's brand, and the scent of a woman.

"This infidelity's got to stop," Arlene told her husband. She wanted the marriage to be a success, thought he did too. But Tommy continued drinking and chasing women. Arlene decided to bide her time and await his transfer back East.

In 1948, Tommy was assigned to two years' shore duty in Norfolk, Virginia. At last he would be close to home. They put their name on the waiting list for military housing, but Arlene preferred the suburbs and the privacy of living off base. They found a small trailer in nearby Little Creek and set up house.

Finally, the marriage seemed stable. Arlene was diagnosed as having a cyst on her womb that prevented her carrying a child to term. She had it removed, and soon after she became pregnant. When Tommy realized the pregnancy was going to term, he balked. The thought of becoming a father made him very nervous.

Arlene's mother sent fourteen-year-old Willie

May to stay with the Kirbys during Arlene's final stage of pregnancy. On July 10, 1949, Belynda Kirby was born at Norfolk Naval Hospital. The little girl was Tommy's pride. Arlene, too, was pleased with her blond baby. She treated her like a little doll, dressed her up in lovely clothes she made and paraded her around Little Creek.

But when Belynda cried, Willie May saw a side of her sister that frightened her. Arlene would scream, "Shut up!" and spank the baby. No, not spank her, Willie May would recall, more like beat her. "She acted like she was a madwoman. What Mother had done was nothing compared to what Myrtle Arlene did to her own daughter."

A year later, Joel Thomas Kirby was born. Tommy was delighted with his son, but Arlene seemed to resent the added burden. Willie May recalled her sister beating both children until their little legs were red from the prints of her hand. Sometimes she hit them with the heel of her shoe. Willie May wrote to Clara that she was scared of their older sister.

Shortly after Joel's birth, Willie May took a daytime baby-sitting job at a neighbor's trailer. In the late afternoon she would return to the Kirby trailer to clean, cook supper, and help with the babies.

In April 1950, Willie May met her future husband, Floyd Heesh. A third-class shipman from Binghamton, New York, Floyd was a friend of Tommy's. Floyd was disturbed by the responsibilities Willie May assumed at the Kirby household and told her so. He gave his girlfriend food money to help out, only to learn that Arlene purchased pork chops and melon for herself, but only cans of pork and beans for Willie May and the children.

Joel was three months old when the Korean War broke out. Tommy was shipped to the Pacific, and Arlene and Willie May took the two babies back to Rossville.

After Willie May's marriage to Floyd in April 1951, she moved to his parents' home in Binghamton, New York, to wait out the war. Arlene found a job first at Davenport Hosiery in Rossville, running the knitting machines that made nylon stockings, then at DuPont as a spinner.

For a short time she and her children lived in the Porter home. But Clard Porter had begun drinking, and the atmosphere was tense. Clara remembered, "Daddy told Mother he would never quit drinking. It was a way of life for him. He got in with this bad family of bootleggers, made their own whiskey, low people who went to square dances. Ain't nothing wrong with a square dance if it's conducted right and people conduct themselves right. It didn't work that way. But Daddy loved to dance." The Porters would divorce within the year, and Esther would marry six more times.

Since moving to Rossville, Arlene's patience with her children had thinned. Tommy was just as intolerant. Both parents had fierce tempers. When he was nine months old, Joel was hospitalized for a bronchial illness, then released while Tommy was on leave. Clara and her father, Clard, were present one night when the couple whipped the child. "Yessir," Clara would recall, "Daddy stopped 'em. He jumped on her and him both for whipping Joel. Daddy knew how they done them babies when they were in the house with him. He'd sat down many a time and cried his eyes out at the way she done them kids."

But there was no telling Myrtle Arlene what to do.

Arlene left the Porter family home and rented a room for herself on Rowland Street, one house away from Clara. In 1948, when she was sixteen, Clara had married David Huskey, a local boy whose family were moonshiners from backwoods Wares Valley, Tennessee, in the heart of the Smoky Mountains. By the time Arlene had returned with her two babies to Rossville, Clara had two children of her own and was expecting another. She would have five in five years.

Still, Clara took Belynda and Joel in, kept

them twenty-four hours a day, seven days a week. "Myrtle Arlene never picked them up but once every two weeks for an hour or so," Clara said. "She was living in nothing but a one-room pigsty, came and went as she pleased, gave no mind to those kids at all."

All the money Arlene was earning at DuPont went toward new clothes. She was a beautiful girl, with thick auburn hair and a slim figure, and she knew how to dress. "Ain't nobody know what I live in," she told her sister Clara. "Don't matter what I live in as long as nobody knows."

One autumn night in October 1951, DuPont gave its annual party for employees. As couples strolled along the banks of the Chattanooga, a riverboat slowly cruised under the moonlight. Marshall Clayburn* had been in Clara's class growing up, and Arlene knew him in passing. He was tall, lean, with thick dark-brown hair and a ready smile.

Clara heard that the two were on the riverboat together. "I can't say whether she was drinking or had a drink, because never in my life have I ever seen or heard of her taking a drink, not even a beer." Several months later Arlene was pregnant. She hurriedly booked a flight to San Diego, where Tommy was stationed. "Takes eight, nine months to have a baby, and Tommy wasn't with her," Clara recalled. "Tommy knew the new baby wasn't his. That boy looked just like Marshall."

When Arlene packed up her children and joined her husband, Clard Porter told Clara, "I see them kids leaving in a casket easier than seeing them leave with her."

Chapter Seven

Belynda Kirby Sabloski's earliest memories are of lions, drunken monkeys, and her family's bungalow collapsing around her.

When she was three, the Kirby family relocated from Rossville to San Diego, then to Alameda, California, near Tommy's base. Joel was two, and Arlene was eight months pregnant with her third child. The house bordered a jungle compound where movie studios trained and housed their animal performers. Many of the captive wildlife were retained for Tarzan movies, the rage of the late forties and fifties.

One evening, fifty white-faced capuchin monkeys broke out of their cages and raucously found their way into a neighbor's vineyard. There they proceeded to fall into one of the wine vats. Belynda watched, laughing, as the jungle workers scurried around, picking up those drunk little monkeys by their tails and stuffing them, headfirst, into sacks.

Her father scooped her up in his arms so she could see better. "They're so drunk they can't even stand up straight," Tommy told his daughter. He was laughing, too.

The first few months in Oakland were a magical time for Belynda. Strange and wonderful creatures inhabited her dreams. Her father played guitar and sang to her. She was daddy's little girl. He'd rock her and she'd fall asleep in his arms, listening to lions roar and the sweet, high-pitched chatter of monkeys.

Because the days were balmy, she and Joel often played on the screened porch. Belynda felt a sense of security she would never know again.

Family histories tend to repeat themselves. Future generations seem bound to inherit their predecessors' particular dances of intimacy and estrangement. Belynda's childhood would bear an eerie resemblance to her mother's—the same fleeting closeness with her father, estrangement from her siblings, and loneliness. But there would be a significant difference in the level of child abuse. Discipline in the Kirby household far exceeded that in the Porter home.

In late May 1952, Alameda was rocked by an earthquake. Belynda was sitting on a kitchen stool when she heard the explosion, a guttural roar, and she felt the wood floor crack beneath her. The bungalow toppled off its foundation, and she was catapulted into the living room. The earthquake predated, by only weeks, a profound shift in her parents' relationship. The quake would become a metaphor for the schism that occurred with the birth of Belynda's second brother, Frederick Wade, in mid-June.

Even as a child Belynda noticed the change in her parents after Wade's birth. The times alone with her father were fewer, and he seemed distracted, angry. At best, Mom ignored her and Joel. At worst, she screamed and hit them. By the time Belynda was five, she was convinced that "my mother hated me being around."

When she was six, the family moved again, this time to New York, where Tommy was assigned to duty at the Brooklyn Navy Yard. They rented an apartment in Queens; the arguments worsened. Mostly they fought about Wade. Tommy did not believe the dark-haired boy was his.

"He don't look like me one bit," Tommy would tell his wife. "And he don't look like them other kids we got."

"You know damn well, Tom Kirby, I was too busy working and taking care of my babies to do any fooling around."

"That kid ain't mine, no way!"

Then he would hit her. Sometimes he'd approach her as if he were going to embrace her. Then he'd haul off and punch her.

During those fights Belynda cowered in her bedroom, her arms wrapped tightly around Joel. But as much as the marital battles frightened her, she dreaded their aftermath even more. When the screaming was over, Tommy went off by himself to drink. Belynda was left alone with a woman who terrified her.

The six-year-old would sneak out of the house and go looking for her father. Invariably, she would find him at one of the neighborhood bars, slumped on a stool. She'd pull on his sleeve and ask him to please come home. He wasn't mean when he drank, but still it was a horrible, dirty feeling, helping him stagger home. He was a big man, and she was afraid he'd fall down and she wouldn't be able to get him back up. He couldn't even walk straight. Sometimes Joel would come along and help her bring him home.

Often Tommy took out his anger directly on Wade. While on a visit to the Kirby home, Clara Huskey did not see Tommy beat Arlene, but she did witness his treatment of the little boy. She watched, horrified, as Tommy strapped the toddler for no reason at all. When the boy screamed in terror, Clara cried out, "Tommy Lee, stop! Don't lay another hand on that child."

"He ain't mine," Tommy said.

"That don't make no difference whether he's yours. The child didn't ask to be born, and he's not here to be mistreated. You're not to touch him again."

Although Tommy was harsh with Wade, he was gentle with his daughter. He protected her from her mother. But that barrier of safety shattered one autumn night in 1956, when Belynda was seven years old. She was in her bedroom when she heard screams, then bumping noises and glass crashing. Suddenly it was quiet. She cautiously stepped into the hallway. The picture window had been smashed; only fragments of glass etched the windowsill. There were police sirens and the red whirring lights of an ambulance.

With a feeling of utter despair Belynda watched her father taken away. Her mother was shouting by the window, through which she had pitched him. "Your daddy's a drunk," Arlene told her children. "He tried to choke me in my sleep." He would never return. A year later, Arlene would tell Belynda, Joel, and Wade that their father was dead.

Soon after Tommy's departure, Arlene was hired as a girl Friday by Seaboard Western Airlines, a cargo company at Idlewild (now Kennedy) Airport in Flushing. By working evening shifts, she could spend her days with her children.

As Arlene remembered, she had no interest in a social life. Her youngsters were enough. When she got off work, her destination was home, no stops along the way.

Arlene's returning to work meant her young daughter had to assume most of the household duties. Arlene slept late in the mornings, and as Belynda recalled, often would go out after work. In the mornings Belynda woke her brothers up, made sure they were properly dressed and had their milk and cornbread for breakfast, got Joel off to school and Wade to his baby-sitter. By the time they returned home, Arlene had already left for work. Belynda gave the boys dinner—a can of beans or soup; then she cleaned the apartment. A neighbor came by to put them to bed but returned at night to her own home and children.

Belynda's diligence notwithstanding, she was increasingly the target of her mother's rages. For a short period, Arlene punished her children by scattering rice pellets on the floor and forcing Belynda, and often Joel, to kneel on the rice for as long as half an hour. The offense could have been something as trivial as forgetting to put the lid on the butter dish. Wade was too little to experience the cruelty of that punishment, how bony knees felt impaled on those pellets; he would just toss about in the rice and laugh.

Still, Arlene preferred the belt to the rice, and whipped it out at any provocation. Belynda would later recall that one of the most terrifying incidents began with a nutrition sheet that her teacher and Joel's had handed out. "I want you to go through the list and check off what you had for breakfast," they told their second and third graders. A healthy breakfast meant you would get a star. The Kirby children were too ashamed to admit their breakfast had been only milk and bread. Belynda wrote that she had eggs, toast, and orange juice; Joel, pancakes and sausage.

Soon after, Arlene received a letter from one of the teachers, who sensed the children had, in fact, eaten poorly.

That evening Arlene whipped Belynda and Joel until she drew blood.

From that day on, Belynda rehearsed with Joel as they walked to school: "Now, what did we have for breakfast? No, you can't say bread and milk. We had cereal and juice."

Other times they had no idea why they were beaten. The offense could have occurred hours, even days earlier. A food stain on their clothes, a look that made Mom mad, one mistake and "the fear of God had better be in you."

Lying awake at night while her mother was at work, Belynda savored those quiet hours. When Mom wasn't home, no one was getting beaten. In the darkness Belynda would summon up happier times. If she shut her mind to the city noises, she could almost hear the drunken monkeys chatter and the lions roar.

But daylight brought a harsher reality. Her father was gone, and she was abandoned with a monster.

Chapter Eight

In early 1957, Arlene and her children moved to a large rental home in Moriches on eastern Long Island. They were soon joined by Arlene's brother, Johnny Luke Porter, his three young children and his wife, Kate, who was pregnant.

With the move, Arlene's commuting distance to Idlewild Airport lengthened. It was a distance measured not only in miles but in state of mind. Farther from home and those who knew her, Arlene easily transformed herself into the persona she cultivated by dress and mannerisms. The Arlene Kirby who worked for Seaboard Western was a beautiful, independent woman, the very image of Southern charm and graciousness. No one knew she lived in a run-down farmhouse with her "Georgia cracker" brother and their sprawling families, or that as a mother she alternated between terrorizing and neglecting her children.

Arlene was mastering the art of disguise. As she had told her sister Clara years before in Rossville, "Don't matter what I live in as long as nobody knows."

Still, eight-year-old Belynda was in awe of her. Mom smelled of flowers and she always wore jewelry, white gloves, and a hat when she left the house. To her awkward daughter, Arlene was the epitome of magazine elegance.

While Arlene worked, Johnny Luke's wife cared for the six Kirby and Porter children. As Johnny Luke would later recall, "Half the time Arlene was gone I was stuck with them [the children]. We'd look after them to make sure they didn't get out of line." He recalls that Wade was "ornery as hell. Arlene had him spoilt, he was her favorite." Joel and Belynda were good kids, but "they took a lot of blame for things Wade done." Too often Johnny would see his sister use excessive force. "She didn't correct the kids right. She'd beat them with anything she'd get her hands on. Belynda was a pretty, sweet little old girl. Quiet-like." She seemed to Johnny to be singled out by her mother's rough hand, more than was called for.

In the middle of one night, Johnny Luke and his family moved from the house in Moriches to a mobile home in Riverhead, farther east. Arlene was furious. "That's just what his asininity done through the years," she later said. "A thought comes into his mind, he wants to do something and he does not give a tinker's damn what he does to anyone else." Never mind the fact that she had helped him when he needed help, got him a job and an automobile.

For a short time, Arlene shuttled her children to Huntington Station, where an old friend baby-sat them. Often she took them to work at night, although Belynda had no recollection of those trips. During one commute, Arlene's car exploded. She remembered being hospitalized, and then losing her job at the airline.

Soon after, she packed the family's belongings into her '49 Chevy and drove down to Rossville to recuperate at her sister Alice's house.

Her family in Georgia recalled that Arlene dropped her three children off for the summer, but they knew nothing about any accident. Arlene returned to New York and, three months later, the children returned home by plane; Arlene was still working for the airline.

In the summer of 1957, Arlene's sister Clara Huskey and her family were living in Park City, a small Rossville community of modest homes and farmhouses with parcels of several acres. The area had seen numerous Civil War battles. The most devastating had been the Battle of Chickamauga. A Cherokee word meaning "river of death," Chickamauga became known as "the bloodiest day of American history." Nearly 38,000 soldiers died on September 19 and 20, 1863, in the wild, uncultivated terrain that had since become the Huskeys' backyard.

Clara's daughter, Kay, and Belynda were only months apart in age, Belynda the older. Kay had heard about "Arlene's ways," but that summer, she saw how her cousin was treated. One afternoon, as the girls were playing, Arlene lunged at Belynda. She grabbed her by the nape of her neck and lifted her right off the ground. Then she started shaking her.

"You let that child go and don't you ever do anything like that in my house again as long as you live!" Clara shouted. "The child didn't ask for you to do that, but if she needed a whipping, the Lord provides a place for that."

Another vicious incident occurred when, several days later, Willie May arrived from Binghamton with her four children. Kay, Belynda, and Willie May's daughter, Sharon, were playing outside. Sharon, the youngest, needed to use the outhouse, but she wanted someone to clean it first. "You don't clean outhouses," Kay told Sharon. Belynda laughed with Kay at the very idea.

Arlene became enraged. She came up behind Belynda, grabbed her by her ear and yanked out her pierced earring, tearing the earlobe. As the blood ran down Belynda's neck, Arlene laughed.

Kay was horrified. What mother would tear off her child's skin and then laugh about it? Kay had always been wary of her Aunt Myrtle. Now she was afraid—for herself and her cousin Belynda.

In 1959, the Kirbys moved to an apartment in Richmond Hills, Queens, a ten-minute drive to Arlene's new job with American Airlines. She continued to work the night shift, and ten-year-old Belynda remained responsible for Joel, then nine, and Wade, seven, as well as a larger apartment.

Maggots were a constant problem in the boys' room. Joel and Wade wet their bunk beds and, instead of pulling off the soaked sheets, they would throw a towel or blanket on top. Hordes of maggots started festering under those layers of bedding. Arlene knew about them but did not seem to care.

Supervising the boys was also becoming more difficult for Belynda. Wade was now unfettered by his father's rages, and he went wild. For one thing, she couldn't take him into a store. He had "sticky fingers," and by the time he was four, he was picking up anything off the shelves that he could hide in his pocket; he adored little cavalry soldiers, plastic penny items that he wouldn't be allowed to buy. He'd tell his mother the toys were gifts from his "friends." When he was five, a more brazen Wade walked out of a store with eleven cowboy hats. He said someone gave them to him, but a store employee followed him home and Wade was forced to relinquish those "gifts."

Socially, it was an awkward time for Belynda. She was a very pretty, fair-haired girl with long legs and an appealing shyness. But she felt ugly and unwanted. She had few friends and was too ashamed to bring them home. There was no predicting her mother's moods, and the apartment always smelled of the boys' bed-wetting.

One evening in early winter, Willie May and Uncle Floyd stopped by Arlene's apartment. While searching for the building number, they spotted Belynda and the boys in the park. Arlene had left the children, on that cold winter night, unsupervised on the city streets.

Willie May was as stunned when she walked into the apartment. "It was a dump," she recalls. "Dirty dishes on the couch, even in the bathtub. There wasn't a clean dish in that place. No food at all." When she saw the bedding in the boys' room, Willie May remembered a peculiar question Wade had posed during a visit to Rossville. "How come you don't have any worms in your beds, Aunt Clara?" he had asked.

Clara had told Willie May, and they both wondered what the little boy meant. Now Willie May knew.

When Arlene walked in, she was surprised to see her sister. But she had plans for the evening and was not about to stay home. Willie May watched her dress up in expensive clothes. She had a full closet of party dresses, said she was going to a modeling assignment. Model what? Willie May wondered.

Still, Belynda preferred neglect to incessant punishment. One particular incident stands out in her mind. It all started when, on a childish impulse, she put a crabapple in the sugar bowl.

That weekend Arlene awoke late, as usual. She and the children sat down for one of their infrequent breakfasts together. Wade clung to her. He was allowed to; she always pushed Belynda and Joel away.

Arlene was reading the paper when she scooped a teaspoon of sugar from the bowl into her cup. The tiny crabapple plopped into her cup, splattering the coffee onto her robe. She pushed back from the table.

"Who did this?"

No one said a word.

"I want to know who put this apple into the sugar bowl." She looked from one child to the other.

Joel was beginning to tremble.

Arlene went into her bedroom and returned

with her belt. She used a razor straw to sharpen the leather. The belt was ready to draw blood.

Arlene whipped each of the children until Belynda could no longer bear the cries of her brothers. She confessed. Wade and Joel ran into their room, and Belynda was left alone with her mother.

"Mom's face, it was horrible. A snarl, an ugly, horrible snarl. She kicked me, punched, beat me. She didn't stop until her arm got too tired. I couldn't yell. I couldn't cry anymore. I thought, I'm going to die. My mother is going to kill me."

Shortly after Belynda's eleventh birthday, Arlene broke her neck while moving furniture at work. She was hospitalized in a chin-to-hip cast, and for a short time the Kirby children stayed with Johnny Luke and Kate in their trailer on Hubbard Avenue, in Riverhead. Johnny Luke soon after drove them all up to Willie May's house in Binghamton, eight children, two adults, luggage, and food crammed into a beat-up station wagon. Belynda was looking forward to staying with Aunt Willie May. School was about to begin, and Willie May had arranged for the Kirby children to attend in Binghamton.

Willie May immediately recognized that the boys needed medical attention. Joel had severe impetigo on his feet and toes. Wade had a nasty running ear that smelled rancid. Both had exposed sores on their legs and arms. "They were," she recalled, "like street urchins."

At that time Willie May had three young children of her own. The family was struggling on Floyd's income as a contractor. She could feed and clothe all of them, but she needed help to pay the Kirby boys' medical bills. Willie May applied to social services for medical assistance but was denied. The children could only receive assistance if they were not living with relatives. She had no choice but to send the Kirby kids back to Long Island.

From her hospital bed, Arlene arranged to have Belynda and the boys placed in foster homes. Joel and Wade would spend the rest of the year together with a family in Hampton Bays. Belynda was sent to a farmhouse in Mattituck and a woman named Mrs. Smith* who had four foster children and a seventeen-year-old adopted daughter, Debby. One of the children, a four-year-old girl, was emotionally disturbed; she had been sexually abused as an infant. Another boy was retarded.

A tall, thin woman with graying dark hair, Mrs. Smith was not particularly loving, but she was not mean. The house was clean, the children well fed and clothed, and Mrs. Smith never raised her voice or struck her wards. Belynda was astounded.

Two weeks into her stay, a social worker stopped by. It was a familiar checkup procedure for Mrs. Smith, who made her living taking in foster children. That day she introduced as her husband a man Belynda had never seen before.

"How come Mr. Smith lives someplace else?" Belynda asked Debby, the adopted daughter. "Doesn't he like kids?"

Debby shushed her. "That's not Mrs. Smith's husband. It's her brother. But don't you ever tell anybody that."

Smith was in his fifties, small in stature but heavyset, and unmarried. He liked taking the kids to the movies or to his house to look at magazines or play games. Sometimes he would take them for ice cream.

Once he took only Belynda. She was sitting beside him in the car when he reached over and put his hand on her knee. He left his hand there. She knew that wasn't supposed to happen. She made herself small against the passenger door and cried.

But Belynda told no one. Who would have believed her? In any event, she did not want to be taken from Mrs. Smith's home. For the first time in her life she was not responsible for another person. She could be a child. Certainly most of her childhood had been stolen from her.

PART THREE

PART THREE

Chapter Nine

Monday, September 9, 1985

Don Delaney sat at his desk examining three
items he had obtained from the Caris residence
at 40 Adams Lane. Two of those items—letters
from Rosalind to Tony—supported Arlene's confession that she had killed Bob Caris. The third
piece of evidence, perhaps as important as the
weapon Arlene had used to commit the murder,
had been delivered to him late that afternoon by
Belynda Sabloski. It was a brown bottle labeled
"Prince Romanov." That bottle, Delaney felt certain, would secure a conviction against Arlene
Caris of premeditated murder in the second degree, the highest count of murder that can be
charged in the state of New York.

At four that afternoon, as Delaney was con-
cluding his interview of Tony Campanella, Belynda had swung into his office, clearly

unnerved. She had just seen her mother at the Riverhead jail. Arlene had, as he predicted, made a request, the nature of which Belynda explained. It was evident that Belynda was extremely distraught at the mounting evidence, but she was determined to do what was right. "I have always had a healthy respect for the law," Belynda told Delaney. "It saw it broken so much by my family. The idea was 'If you can get away with it, it's okay.' I couldn't live with that guilt. If I don't help you, I would be party to Bob's murder."

Delaney instructed Belynda to comply with her mother's request, except that she was not to dispose of the bottle; she was to bring it to him. It was now on his desk, half full. Several months before the murder, Arlene, it seemed, had begun to poison her husband.

This new information clarified the picture considerably. The shooting had not, in fact, been an isolated event prompted by an impulsive rage. It had simply been Arlene's one successful attempt in a series of unsuccessful attempts to kill Bob Caris. This premeditation eliminated her strongest defense, that of "extreme emotional disturbance."

"Extreme emotional disturbance would have knocked murder second-degree down to manslaughter," Delaney later explained. "The person could allege the murder was a reaction to a heated argument: you lose it and murder someone, no premeditation. That was not the case with Caris's murder. This was not just a one-shot deal, not a result of Arlene's losing her temper because she was a supposedly battered wife."

At Delaney's request, Tony Campanella had also returned to the Caris house to retrieve the letters his wife had written him. The letters did not support premeditation, but they did corroborate the fact that Arlene had killed her husband. The first letter was dated April 7, 1985. In a childish scrawl replete with spelling errors and emphatic underlines, Rosalind told her incarcerated husband what had transpired on the morning of March 29.

At the top of the page, Rosalind had printed in large letters: "<u>I Love You!!</u>"

Dearest Sweet Heart,
It felt so good to hear your voice today. I'm so happy that your out of the <u>Box</u> (happy days). Babe, what I told you today on the phone, isn't a bunch of <u>Bull Shit</u> either, It's the Truth.
Mom got rid of her problem (her husband). Like, I told you, I was a sleep when that Shit went <u>down!!</u> I remember, her waking me up. I ask her, what was wrong? She told me, that we didn't have to worry about asshole anymore. I

said why? Where is he, and that's when she told me that, It (her husband) was gone. Babe, what the <u>Fuck</u> am I gonna do now cause I'm Scared to death!! I hate to ask this question but, will you leave me because of this <u>shit!</u> I already know what the answer is (I hope!) No, right (I hope!).

I couldn't tell you any of this shit, while you were in the box. I had to wait until you called or I saw you. I hope you can understand. <u>Please, help, me, Babe, Please!!</u> I'm going Fuckin' crazy.

Well, besides that everything is OK! Little Bit is missing her daddy very much, and so do I. It shouldn't be to long and I'll be paying my Sweetheart a visit! I can't wait to hold you in my arms again.

Well, I guess that's it for now. I will ask mom about your cassette player, OK!, so Smile for me cause, I Love Ya!

> Love Always,
> For Ever, for Life
> For all Eternity
> Rosalind
> &
> Danielle

Rosalind had been booked on first-degree hindering prosecution, then released. She had agreed to turn state's evidence, and there was no compelling reason to detain her.

Belynda had offered to care for her niece, Danielle, during this crisis period. She allowed Rosalind to stay only one night; neither Fred nor Lori welcomed the wild young woman's presence. That Monday evening, Rosalind had returned to the Sabloski home to put her daughter to bed. The little girl now slept on a pullout couch, hugging her doll, the one Lori had found "in the room next to where Grandpa's stuffed."

Although Rosalind was not detained by the police, she still wasn't in the clear with her sister. Belynda confronted her in the kitchen, but Rosalind brushed her off.

"Why don't you forget about it already?" Rosalind said.

"Is that what you did, Roz? Forget about it. Forget about Dad's body in the attic?"

"He wasn't my dad."

Hours earlier, Belynda had found the bottle labeled "Prince Romanov." It had been hidden behind dishes in the display cabinet where Mom kept the good china.

"Is that why it was okay to poison his food, Roz?"

"His food and tea," Rosalind corrected her.

Belynda felt too exhausted to react. "How long was this going on?"

"A couple months." Rosalind blew smoke rings toward the ceiling.

Belynda knew that Bob and Danielle had often eaten from the same plate, the baby sitting on her grandpa's lap as he fed her. Had Danielle been inadvertently poisoned as well?

Rosalind replied, "Mom wouldn't let Danielle eat from Bob's plate anymore. She gave me money to take her to McDonald's."

"How could you sleep on the same floor where Bob's body was? How could you do that to your own daughter?"

Rosalind flicked her cigarette ash into the sink and said nothing.

Belynda controlled an impulse to slap her sister. "Bob treated you like you were his own daughter. He loved you."

"You don't know anything about it," Rosalind said.

Oh, yes, I do, Belynda thought. I do know about it. She, Lori, and Monica had lived in the Caris home for fourteen months after she left Paul Dubin. She had had no place else to go. The irony of returning to her mother for safety was not lost on Belynda, but she saw Bob Caris as a kind person, someone who really cared. Hopefully with the love of this good man, her mother had changed.

The Caris household Belynda had observed during her stay was a comfortable one. Her mother seemed happy. She had a beautiful home in an expensive neighborhood and a man who clearly adored her. Rosalind did not have to worry about her next meal or having heat in the house or being beaten. Belynda had to admit she was envious of Roz. Her own childhood had been a tortured one, and her marriage to Dubin had violently ended. Nine-year-old Rosalind had what Belynda had always wanted, for herself and her own children.

Rosalind was, indeed, treated like a princess, and she seemed to know how to ensure that such royal treatment continued. The little girl was a skillful manipulator. She had, after all, the best teacher.

What bothered Belynda most was Roz's apparent lack of conscience when she lied, which was frequently and blatantly. She created havoc between Bob and Arlene, yet expressed no guilt at the resulting ill will. Rosalind did what she needed to do to get her way, no matter what harm resulted. Yet Bob Caris never said one negative word about his stepdaughter. Belynda had never heard Bob say anything derogatory about anyone. While Rosalind provoked, Bob tried to keep the peace. "Rosalind needs a little more understanding than most kids," he had once told Belynda.

Belynda had known then that this man really loved Arlene's child.

Now there was another little girl to consider. "Roz," Belynda said. "We need to talk about Danielle. What if she gets sick, or there's a medical emergency and you're not around? I need the authority to act on your behalf. Mom's gone, you don't know where the hell your husband is, you don't have a job. Let me have legal custody of Danielle, at least for now. Until you know what you're going to do." When Rosalind did not respond, Belynda added gently, "She's just another responsibility you don't need now."

"Okay," Rosalind said.

Belynda made a mental note to inquire about the legal papers. At least Danielle would be safe, for a while.

As Rosalind walked out the Sabloskis' front door and into the cool September night, Belynda felt a sudden pang of sadness. Rosalind was as much Mom's victim as she had been.

Chapter Ten

Belynda was twelve years old when Rosalind's father, Bob Lotz, came into their lives. Arlene had been dating on and off, but none of her colleagues at work. They simply did not have the qualifying financial status.

Arlene met Lotz through Parents Without Partners. He was twenty-three years older than she, about five feet four, stocky, with a crew cut. Belynda described him as "very Germanic, very abrupt." Lotz had had a good deal of money, but at least two unsuccessful marriages had depleted his resources. Still, Arlene saw his yacht and country club membership in the prestigious Long Island community of Glen Cove as proof enough of prosperity.

Lotz's lifestyle was certainly more attractive than the trailer park on Hubbard Avenue in Riverhead where, a year earlier, Arlene had installed her family. Johnny Luke also lived in that park with his brood, and Arlene positioned her trailer next to his to share the electric line. She agreed to split the bill at month's end. However, the arrangement soon provoked bitter fights about costs, to the point of physical confrontations between Arlene and Kate. A lot of hair pulling and screaming.

By this time Joel and Wade had become impossible for Belynda to control. Wade had graduated from stealing cowboy hats to breaking into and trashing trailers; he was joined in those pursuits by Joel. Belynda ended up shouldering the blame, and whippings, for her bothers.

As the punishments worsened, enemy camps were created within the Kirby household. The children were on guard against not only their mother, but one another. Survival meant turning in your sibling in order to protect yourself. Whatever camaraderie might have existed in that tortured household had been destroyed; there was no safety even when Arlene was not home.

Belynda's grades were faltering, and her self-image had plummeted to a new low. "How dare you bring home grades like that?" Arlene told her. "You're the daughter of a woman who graduated high school at the age of fourteen and was double-promoted, skipped grades all through school. I was the youngest pupil on campus in college." Arlene never did tell her what college she attended, but Belynda nonetheless felt intimidated. Mom was so smart; what was wrong with her?

Bob Lotz occasionally visited their trailer, but he had little patience for the children. It was his opinion that they should be shipped off to boarding school. So Arlene spent most weekends on his yacht, leaving the boys home in Belynda's care.

To Belynda, her mother seemed timid around Bob Lotz, as if she were afraid of him. As Belynda recalled, "Lotz didn't take any crap. It was his way or no way."

In the summer of 1962, a year after Arlene had started dating Lotz, she moved her family to Goldman's Trailer Park, a nearby mobile home enclave. Arlene wanted to get her children away from Kate Porter, who, she charged, was using the kids as "her servants."

In mid-October, Arlene returned from her usual weekend with Lotz and announced to her children that she and Bob had gotten married. It was time to get on with her life, she said. She had been a "widow," after all, for three years.

Despite the marriage, Lotz did not move into the Kirby trailer, nor did the family move in with him. His visits were, if anything, less frequent, and Arlene spent more time away. She considered thirteen-year-old Belynda, Joel, twelve, and Wade, ten, to be "young adults." She had taught them to take care of themselves. "As far as any supervision, the kids did well on their own. They were damned good kids." She was fortunate.

Nine months later, on July 10, 1963, Rosalind Lotz was born. Coincidentally, Rosalind and her oldest sister shared the same birthday. But in Arlene's eyes Belynda and Rosalind were polar opposites. "Belynda was preciously beautiful. Rosalind was an ugly duckling, nine weeks premature at eight pounds, two ounces. Belynda first saw her little sister in the nursery and she cried, 'She's so ugly!' "

As Arlene recalled, Belynda resented Rosalind early on. While the boys treated their baby sister like a toy, "Belynda was wearing two faces, she was jealous of her. She didn't want me to know she was feeling those things about her. Belynda was the only daughter, the apple of her mother's eye, then Rosalind comes along and her brothers doted on their baby sister. They thought she was the grandest thing next to chocolate pie."

Belynda, though, remembers her own delight at Rosalind's birth. She could not have wished for a better birthday gift. She had "two bratty little brothers," who wouldn't mind her, but now she had a "little baby doll, a live baby doll."

Someone she could love and who would return that love.

By then Arlene was working in the silverware department at Macy's, a managerial job she only temporarily interrupted to give birth. During the day she left Rosalind with a baby-sitter who lived near the trailer court. Belynda would pick her sister up after school and care for her. Even when Mom was home, she was responsible for the baby. "Go ask your sister," Mom would say whenever Roz wanted something. Rosalind called Belynda "Sister," as if it were her proper name, up until she was four years old.

On weekends, Arlene would take Rosalind to stay on Lotz's boat. Belynda and her brothers remained behind.

It was a precarious time for the fourteen-year-old. Belynda had reached puberty early, but she was emotionally still a child. At home she was made to feel ugly, unwanted, but in school she drew the attention and teasing of the boys. She was a very pretty teen, a full-figured five two, with dirty-blond hair, a tiny waist, and developed breasts that she tried to conceal. She was saving her baby-sitting money to buy clothes like the other kids wore, instead of the sheer blouses her mother bought her. Self-conscious about her maturing body, Belynda made sure never to wear low-buttoned blouses or pullover sweaters.

There were two cliques at Riverhead Junior High: the greasers and the collegiates. Greaser boys were the "hoods." They wore slicked-back pompadours, white button-down shirts, black chino pants that stopped at the ankle, leather "shitkicker" boots, and leather jackets. Their greaser girlfriends high-teased and sprayed their hair, wore very short, tight skirts, black fishnets and high heels, and always a lot of makeup. Belynda tended more toward the "madras" look of the collegiate girls, but she was drawn to the greaser boys. They were more exciting and had nicer cars.

In any event, she kept her distance. She desperately wanted a boyfriend, but she was afraid. Boys were like a flame. If you got too close, you got burned.

Inviting any of her friends to her trailer was out of the question. It wasn't dirty—she saw to its cleanliness—but it smelled of urine. Arlene had to purchase two new mattresses every year because of the boys' chronic bed-wetting. Years later, Joel would be discharged from the military for medical reasons: he still wet his bed.

Over everything loomed the specter of her mother. Belynda remembers one brief interlude where Arlene cajoled her into stealing.

For several weeks, Arlene was bringing home expensive pieces of silverware from her department at Macy's. On the weekends she would drive her daughter to various Macy's stores to return the items for cash refund. Sterling silver, sometimes a thirty-five- or forty-eight-piece set, returned for cash using sales slips that Arlene phonied up. She would go through the phone book, pick out a name and tell Belynda to memorize the address and phone number. "Don't give them your real name, don't ever tell them your real name. If they act suspicious, just leave."

Belynda's heart beat so fast that she barely managed to give any name at all. After several weekends of returning merchandise, she froze at the counter one afternoon. No sound came out of her mouth. The saleswoman stared suspiciously at her. Belynda bolted, crying, from the store and flung herself into her mother's waiting car. In the close space she felt that she was suffocating. She was going crazy.

Mother and daughter never spoke about the incident, but the silverware returns stopped.

This humiliation was followed by others. Experimenting with new hairstyles was certainly not a novel pastime among teenage girls. That year the French twist was all the rage of her collegiate girlfriends; it was also a style Arlene had long fancied for herself. Belynda had always admired her mother's rich auburn hair pinned up in the meticulous style. She thought Mom would feel complimented if she, too, wore a twist. It would be something they shared.

When Arlene saw her daughter fussing with her hair, she warned, "If I catch you teasing your rat hair like that, I'm going to cut it off."

Belynda took her mother's threat lightly. The welts from the beatings could be hidden by clothing, but Mom's cutting her hair off would be too visible an outrage. Everyone would see how cruel she really was. Arlene could not risk so public a display of brutality.

Belynda continued to set her hair in large rollers, tease it and twist it, and bask in her schoolmates' compliments. But she made sure to brush it out before her mother came home from work. One afternoon Arlene returned unexpectedly early. Belynda's hair was still pinned up, but Arlene said nothing about it. That evening, she made her daughter a cup of hot chocolate. Belynda sat in bed sipping the treat, surprised but delighted by her mother's unexpected kindness. She slept heavily that night.

The following morning, Arlene was in the kitchen when she heard Belynda's bloodcurdling scream. Her long blond hair, still bound in rollers, lay on the pillow, severed from her head. Bald spots peppered her scalp where her mother had clipped the hair too close. She broke into hysterical sobs. In the kitchen Arlene was laughing.

Arlene was still laughing when she told Willie May about the incident. What kind of monster are you that you could do your child that way? Willie May thought to herself. But you didn't tell Myrtle Arlene, that's not right. She would just turn her anger on the kids.

When Rosalind was nine months old, Arlene's trailer was repossessed, and the family moved with Bob Lotz to a house in Lake Ronkonkoma. Lotz immediately laid down the rules: the house must be kept immaculate, and the adults' bedroom was off-limits to the children. He would not tolerate the smell of urine in the house, so Wade and Joel slept in the unfinished, unheated basement. Plastic sheets covered the boys' beds; Lotz made sure they were changed daily.

Arlene delighted in her husband's initial fascination with his daughter. "At first he was in awe of her, like he couldn't believe this little person was created by him. Not that he ever thought she wasn't his, more like disbelief that at his age he could have a child." Rosalind toddled after her daddy like, Arlene said, "a little shadow."

Arlene was happy. She had found in Bob Lotz her match. And on no subject were they more in agreement than on the topic of corporal punishment. Together they devised Arlene's punitive instrument of choice, a cat-o'-nine tails.

To make the whip, Arlene took two strips of leather, two inches wide, a half-inch thick and three feet long, and soaked them in oil to soften them. Then she nailed the tops of those pieces to the front and back of a wooden board that was about three inches wide and one inch thick. She used a razor blade to cut the strips into nine "tails." By the time she was finished, there were eighteen leather strips. Lotz then lacquered the handle to a fine amber gloss.

As Belynda recalls, the cat-o'-nine-tails slit the skin like razor blades, tore the flesh right off your body, just ripped it off, ripped you wide open.

Sometimes Belynda got so angry at the whippings, she wanted to really hurt her mother, hurt her bad. She'd do anything just to make her stop. But that scared her. Maybe the evil that was in her mother was in her, too.

Often she thought of running away. But where would she go? How would she get there? What would she do to keep herself alive? And there were her brothers and her little sister. She had to at least try to protect them.

The violence was not all directed at the children, however. Belynda was in her bedroom one evening when she heard shots. She went flying down the hall to the kitchen where her mother and Lotz were screaming, rolling around the floor. He had a gun in his hand. It fired twice. A neighbor must have called the police because within minutes they were at the door. Belynda saw Lotz flash them what looked like a badge. He told the cops he was a deputy sheriff. He said, "This is not a domestic dispute. This is a common-law marriage, just living with her common-law." Lotz promised there would be no more violence that night. The cops left without even taking the gun.

The incident was prompted by Arlene's confronting Lotz about the status of their marriage. To her surprise, she learned she was not legally married.

"I was married on October 15, 1962, in Huntington, of all things, I found out, by a defrocked minister, and the marriage was never recorded. It wasn't worth the paper it was written on. He once made a statement to my older kids, 'Well, you know your mother and I aren't married, just shacking up.' I had a piece of paper that all it needed for a marriage certificate was a New York State seal. I hadn't looked at it that close. When he made that statement, I went looking for it. And there was no seal on it! I didn't try to get married to him because by then I didn't want to be married to the man."

Still, Arlene stayed, as yet other gunfights

blasted holes in the walls and ceilings, and the police continued to make routine calls to the Lotz residence. It was not until the following year when Lotz attacked Belynda that Arlene finally sent him packing.

Early the summer of Belynda's sixteenth birthday, she broke her neck diving into a neighbor's swimming pool. She was hospitalized for two months and returned home wearing a cervical collar; she was in traction four hours a day. One afternoon, Belynda was gazing out the living room window watching her mother and Bob Lotz in the backyard when she saw him suddenly punch Arlene in the chest. He kept on hitting her and shouting. Belynda hurled herself outside, screaming for him to stop. Lotz swung around and punched her in the face. Belynda fell to the ground. He kicked her until she was unconscious. Several hours later she awoke in Smithtown General Hospital with no feeling in her neck and two broken ribs. For another two weeks, she remained under observation.

Arlene told Lotz to leave—permanently. Yet they continued dating for two more years, right up until he had a fatal heart attack.

Years after his death, Arlene was still fuming about the illicit union. "To think that I had been used in such way as that, taken advantage of. To me that was one of the most despicable things that I had ever encountered. I was so mad I felt like plunging a knife through him."

In Her Own Words: Arlene Caris

I met Bob Lotz in 1961. I was introduced to him by a mutual friend who was living in Huntington Station. I was living in Riverhead. I had a mobile home out in the area, and I was commuting from Riverhead to Idlewild every day. When I first met him, I didn't think one way or another. I wasn't looking for a relationship. I had my three kids, I had my job. And that's all I concentrated on.

He was a neat type of person. He knew how to behave like a gentleman. He treated me like a lady. God only knows if he was divorced or not. He said he was. That was about his third or fourth, I'm not sure. I didn't start dating him right away. I wasn't looking for that type of a relationship. It seems whenever I'd be at my friend Miriam's place he'd either be there or show up shortly after. We'd get to talking. One thing led to another. I agreed to go out with him. I knew him about a year and a half before I agreed to be his wife.

If ever a man had a woman on a pedestal, he had me there. There wasn't anything too good for me. He liked to go out to dinner. He liked a genteel type of social entertaining. And then, too, he had a very nice place. All the little niceties. Anything a woman could ask for. He had some money in the bank. He was not an extremely wealthy man. I was not looking for a wealthy man. I was just looking for the good in the person. I took him at face value only to find out I couldn't take him as such.

I didn't feel any phoniness during the dating relationship. It was after I thought I was married to him that it was Jekyll and Hyde. Once the commitment was made, I didn't even know him. If he had shown that nastiness, meanness, that abusive side of himself to me, I would have walked immediately.

At one time, he had started with his, I called it, "his thinking thinkin'." Lotz was a terribly jealous person. All I had to do, the mailbox was right out front the entry door, and if I happened to go to the mailbox the same time the postman was coming up the walkway, he had me in bed with the postman. I didn't even know what the postman's name was.

At first he welcomed the idea of having another family. After he found out I was expecting Rosalind, it was a different tune. He started being nasty and obnoxious to the others.

A good example [was] Father's Day before

Rosalind was born. The three kids had pooled their money, resources, and bought him a nice Old Spice shaving kit. When they gave it to him the morning of Father's Day, he looked at it and went right to the door of the trailer and threw it out the door. He wasn't their father. He didn't want anything from them. Absolutely broke their hearts. I had one of them go out and pick up the package and bring it inside. I took a look at it afterwards to see if anything was damaged. I told him, "It's time you left right now."

That was June 1963, before she was born in July.

I was still working at Macy's during my pregnancy. I took time out to have her and I was right back.

We were in a Chinese restaurant in Huntington one night. He had taken some papers out of his inside coat pocket, told me he had some papers he wanted me to sign for financing his boat. I said, "You financed that boat before you ever knew me and you didn't need my signature then. Why would you need it now?"

He had a funny look on his face. I started reading those papers. They were adoption papers. He was giving the baby away, but he couldn't do it without my signature. I looked at him and I dumped that table right in his lap right then and there.

"You don't give away this baby. You don't have final say to it. I have something to say about it."

He thought he was getting a little too old for that sort of thing.

I told him, "You should have thought about this before. We talked about this before we decided to make our lives together."

Mr. and Mrs. Lee intervened. He came over, the owner of the restaurant, and ushered me into his office where Mrs. Lee took over and insisted I sit down and have a cup of tea and tell her what it was all about. The proprietor took care of him. One of them drove me back over to Macy's because I was only on my lunch hour.

I had her three days later.

We had an eat-in type of kitchen and he had his guns out. I always thought he was rather careless with them. He had several. I was sitting across the table from him. Rosalind was about two years old. He pointed the gun at me and accused me of having these affairs.

I said, "When do I have time for these things you accuse me of? I go to work, and you know I get home a few minutes before you do and by the time you get here I have the table set and supper almost ready to put on the table. Now when am I supposed to have time for any of these accusations?"

I know exactly what kind of gun it was. It was a police special. He was close with a sheriff at the time. All he had to do was make application for whatever gun permits he wanted and he had no problems getting them.

He was cleaning the gun and he pointed it at me. I knew the son-of-a-gun was going to pull the trigger at me. When I saw his finger tighten on the trigger, I ducked, pushed the table into him and I pushed him with all my might. When the table hit, he went over backward. He fired the gun and the bullet went so close to my head I could feel the heat of the whistle from it, the motion from it.

The kids were in the house. The two boys were downstairs. Belynda was in her room. Rosalind was probably in her little room. They were petrified. They didn't know what to do. When I pushed the table into him he still managed to squeeze another shot, which went into the ceiling. I jumped over the table, and I stomped on his hand, kicked the gun out of his hand, picked it up, emptied the bullets out of the chamber and pistol-whipped him with his own damn gun. But when he saw I emptied the chamber, he tried to attack me. I wouldn't have hit him with his gun but he made a lunge for me physically. When he did, I let him have it at the side of his head with his own gun.

When he saw his head was bleeding—somebody else's blood didn't bother him, but his *own* head—he asked me to take him to the doctor and get stitches. I said, "Well, you'll get the stitches but I'm not taking you anywhere. You have a car out here. You know where the emergency room is in the hospital, so take care of what has to be taken care of. You had no call to point that gun at me, let alone pull the trigger. You knew perfectly well what you were doing. I don't understand a man like you at all."

I don't know whether I chase them or they chase me. I know what they say attracted them to me, the fact that I was independent, standing on my own two feet, making my own decisions. And this was was something they resented in me, and they wanted to break me. They wanted to break my spirit. That's exactly what they wanted.

Chapter Eleven

San Francisco
Saturday, September 14, 1985

For most of the afternoon, Bob Caris's adopted daughter Sharon Wheeler had been preoccupied with her eldest son, Bill. His depressions, which had begun shortly after the breakup of his parents' marriage, had worsened. He was a gifted young man, always had excelled academically, and his charm and good looks had won him numerous friends. But lately Sharon had seen a visible change in him. Bill was withdrawing from the world into a place where no one, not even she, could reach him.

Sharon felt frightened and helpless and so needy herself. Nothing had prepared her for the collapse of her life.

There was still no word from her father. Regardless of when she called, Arlene said she had "just missed him. You mean he still has not written?" The excuses her father's wife made over the phone and in her letters were utterly improbable. More disturbing to Sharon were the resentment and rage Arlene appeared to harbor toward Bob Caris and men in general.

In a January letter, Arlene had encouraged Sharon not to give her husband a divorce: "Let Earl know what it feels like for you to tell him to go take a good, healthy crap in his hat and pull it right down over his ears." Arlene wrote that she was furious at her own husband's decision to retire and the loss of income, and at his criticism of Rosalind, which was destroying her loving relationship with her daughter.

Sharon knew her father was disappointed in Rosalind. He had had such high hopes for his new "little girl." But Sharon could not conceive of her mild-mannered father pitting one family member against the other. Arlene's choice of words to defend Rosalind greatly distressed Sharon. "When I saw what was being tried on me and my daughter, I let go both barrels," Arlene wrote.

Sharon often thought about that peculiar phrase, couched as it was in a letter seething with frustration, one that spoke of "a world gone mad, at least the male population." Sharon told a close friend, a superintendent of a local school district, "Either my dad is senile or she murdered him."

At four o'clock Sharon poured herself a cup of coffee and sat down at the kitchen table. Just then the phone rang.

"Is this Sharon Wheeler?" The man's voice on the other end had a distinct New York accent.

"Yes, it is."

He introduced himself as Tom Hall, an attorney retained by Belynda Sabloski, who was now in his office.

"Is there someone there with you, Mrs. Wheeler?" he asked.

"No."

"You need to sit down," Hall told her.

"This is about my dad, isn't it?" Sharon said. "He's been murdered and it's my stepmother who did it."

Every Sunday, Fred Sabloski drove to the 7-Eleven convenience store at the corner of County Road 39 and North Sea Road in Southampton. There he purchased a *New York Daily News* and a cup of coffee, light with two sugars. He would return to his truck, immediately flip to the sports page, and sit there reading and drinking his coffee. It was a long-standing weekend ritual that Lori described as "time for Dad to get away from the four crazy women in his house."

The week of September 8, the Sabloski family clung desperately to its old routines, hoping to palliate the chaos now at the center of their lives. On that Sunday morning Lori, too, stopped at 7-Eleven on her way to hockey practice. She knew her father would be there, and she was hoping to speak with him.

No one could talk at home. Anything sent her mother into hysterics. Everyone else had to be strong. The responsibility for running the house was left to her and her father. Lori was angry at her mother for her inability to control herself, and she was enraged at her grandmother for plunging the Sabloski family into the Caris nightmare.

Lori had retained her biological father's surname, Marena,* and only a few close friends knew that Bob Caris was her grandfather. She had heard the cruel jokes among her unsuspecting classmates and customers at the video store and BK's Restaurant, where she worked part-time. Everyone seemed to be talking about "the body in the closet." She had run crying from her mechanical drawing class when she overheard a student remark: "Imagine living in that house—the smell!"

The headlines smeared across the New York

City papers were bad enough, but Lori was particularly angered by the local press. The descriptions of her grandparents were patently absurd. The *Southampton Press* reported: "Described by one neighbor as a 'wiseguy' and a 'macho guy,' Mr. Caris allegedly drove his wife to murder by 'continually picking on [her] and pushing [her] around.'"

Grandpa, a macho wiseguy? Grandma, pushed around? Lori alternated between tears and laughter at the absurd portrayal.

When she had gone to 40 Adams Lane with Fred and the police and seen the air fresheners lining the attic stairs, Lori felt a terrifying sense of déjà vu. A few days before her grandfather's body was found, she had a dream: Grandpa had fallen down the stairs, and he was dead. He was lying dead in the house.

From the time Lori was five, she associated her grandfather with stairs. Always, she was told: "Be very quiet going down the stairs to see Grandpa." Often, she stood at the head of the basement stairs, listening to his soft voice as he talked into his ham radio. She thought of Grandpa as a nice man, the "Man in the Basement," but even as she got older he remained a shadowy, albeit kindly, presence.

It was Grandma who dominated the house, whom everyone *had* to like better than anyone else. Grandma controlled everybody. At first Lori had been scared of her. But soon she hated her. If there was such a thing as the devil, it was Grandma Arlene.

But no one had remotely suspected that Arlene had killed her husband. Who wanted to believe they had a murderer in their family? Of course there was Uncle Wade, but he was a distant figure. Besides, Wade had been in jail almost all his life. Lori had not lived with him or sat across the table from him, and he had not tried, intentionally, to destroy her life. It was Arlene, not Wade, who had told her that her real father, Joe Marena, wanted nothing to do with her.

Lori thought of all the times she had fought with her grandmother, had openly wished her dead. "I'll dance on your grave," Lori told her the last time they had seen each other. If Grandma was crazy enough to kill her husband, why not her grandchild?

This Sunday morning Lori pulled into the 7-Eleven parking lot, a few spaces from Fred's truck. She saw his head bent over the paper, and she felt grateful for his preserving the Sunday morning ritual amid all this turmoil.

Lori was walking to his passenger window when she stopped short. Her father was crying. She had never seen him cry. He was reading the paper, and his chest was heaving in sobs. She knew he had not seen her. "Mr. Fred" would not want her to see him bawling like this.

The numbness Lori had felt all week broke, and her heart lurched with pain. She had never loved good, kind Fred more than she did at that moment, nor felt more separate from him. He was the only father she had known, but she did not have his blood running through her veins. Arlene Caris was her own flesh and blood, and Arlene had killed another human being. If that evil something is in your genes, Lori wondered then, what does that make me?

With the wisdom that tragedy sometimes evokes in the young, Lori knew her mother must be tormented by an even more terrifying question. What if it were your own mother who had killed someone, what would that make you?

Becoming a mother was the furthest thing from Belynda's mind when she was a senior in high school. But she was lonely and vulnerable and anxious to escape her mother.

In 1965, shortly after Lotz's attack on Belynda sent her to the hospital, Arlene moved her family to a cheaper rental property on Iroquois Street. Belynda was seventeen. That year she fell in love with Victor Esta,* a former classmate and neighbor who had since joined the Navy. She had had one boyfriend before Esta, Dan Wheaton,* a junior high classmate. They began dating when she was fourteen, which meant going to the movies and holding hands. For two years they were inseparable and Belynda was warmly accepted into the Wheaton family. One night they made love. They hadn't planned to, it just happened, and it surprised them both. The romance ended amicably, when each went to different high schools.

Esta was eighteen, and it felt to Belynda like a grown-up relationship. He was sent to boot camp in the Great Lakes, and when he and Belynda were reunited during his first leave, they became engaged. On his second leave, though, Victor returned with a young woman from Chicago whom he had just married. Belynda fell into a deep depression.

"Listen to me next time and you won't lose your man," Arlene told her.

Joe Marena, a neighbor, was about eight years older than Belynda. He had two small children and was working as a builder. Arlene was consulting him on some renovations to her house, and when he came by, he would stay a while to chat with Belynda. Arlene could see that Marena found her daughter attractive, and she encouraged him to visit.

"He's not some snot-nosed kid," she told Belynda.

But wasn't he married?

"Ellie? She means nothing to him. She's no good for him. You play your cards right, you can get him."

Arlene and Ellie had become good friends, but Belynda disliked her from the start. Ellie Marena* was abrasive and crude, a screamer whose shrill voice was familiar to all the neighbors. "Ellie mistreats him," Arlene told her daughter. "She doesn't know what a good person Joe is."

Arlene was working two jobs and dating a widower named Frank McDonald,* whom she had met like Lotz, at a Parents Without Partners meeting, and so she was rarely home. Soon Marena began coming just to see Belynda. At first the relationship was platonic. They just talked. Joe was very nice, and Belynda didn't want to be alone.

He told Belynda that he was not married. He was, he said, only living with Ellie. Belynda thought he was a nice man, a sympathetic listener. Then one day he kissed her, and it felt so comfortable, so right. Soon she fell in love with him.

On weekends, Arlene would drive her daughter to motels to meet Marena. "He's a good catch," Arlene kept reminding Belynda. "He's got a good income, he's a hard worker, he has his own business. If you get pregnant, he'll marry you."

In August, Belynda learned she was pregnant. She wrote to her cousin Kay that she had met a wonderful man who loved her and promised to take care of her. She did not mention that Marena was living with another woman or that she was pregnant.

Kay was overjoyed. Belynda had often told her, "All I want, Kay, is for someone to put his arms around me and tell me he loves me." Finally, Belynda had found love, and she could escape Arlene.

Belynda, however, became severely depressed. She had never been a particularly good student, but she did excel in one program: DECA, Distributive Education Club of America, which prepared students who had decorative arts and business abilities to become entrepreneurs; she had looked forward to a career. Her teacher, Kenneth Nokar, made her feel she was worth something. "You can run your own business one day," he told her. In her senior year she was named Miss DECA Sweetheart.

Mr. Nokar encouraged her to go to business college, but she could not afford the tuition. She had her sights set on joining the Navy, where she would be guaranteed room and board and schooling.

Now she was going to be an unwed mother, pregnant by a man who she suspected was married—despite his protestations to the contrary. Abortion was illegal. She could give the baby away. She knew, though, she could not part with her own flesh and blood.

Mr. Nokar was devastated when she told him she was pregnant. "You don't know what you've done to your future," he said.

At first Marena was sympathetic, protective. He promised to marry her. In mid-September, Arlene drove her daughter to exit 62 on the Long Island Expressway, where Joe was waiting. He and Belynda continued south toward Maryland, where they intended to be married.

En route Belynda had second thoughts. What if Joe were still married? He could go to jail for bigamy. She didn't want her baby to begin life like this. She blurted out, "I need to know whether you are married to Ellie or not. I'm not going to marry you until I know for sure."

Marena veered off the interstate and slammed on the brakes. "Then you have a real serious problem," he said.

Belynda could not understand his sudden rage; it terrified her in the way her mother's anger had. Marena turned the car around and headed back in silence.

When they arrived in Lake Ronkonkoma it was

dark. Arlene had already told Ellie that Joe had gone off and married Belynda. The next morning Ellie Marena appeared at her doorstep, screaming, "You fucking little whore. You broke up my marriage!" Belynda could not leave her house without Ellie assaulting her with obscenities.

Marena would remain with his wife for several more years, but he and Belynda never spoke.

Meanwhile, Arlene gloated: Belynda couldn't even get the father of her baby to marry her.

After the thwarted elopement, Belynda wrote to Kay that her new husband had been sent to Vietnam.

The family in Georgia was doubtful. Wait, Clara told her own daughter Kay. Next you'll hear she's pregnant and her husband got killed in Vietnam. It's just Myrtle's way of covering up.

As the family predicted, Belynda soon wrote that she was pregnant. Arlene followed up with yet more news: Belynda's husband, the father of her baby, had just been killed in Vietnam.

Belynda's due date was May, but she was still determined to graduate that month with her class. Arlene told her to forget about finishing school. What did she need a degree for, anyway? Joel, with all his intelligence and promise, had quit when he was sixteen, bored and impatient to be on his own. He had taken odd jobs, mostly as a mechanic, earned enough to travel the country, then returned home when his money ran out. Joel had always been a silent observer, never one to offer information about himself, but he tried to be kind to Belynda. Not like Wade. Wade would deliberately destroy anything he felt was of value to another person. Wade was sixteen when he racked up his first serious offense: burglary. Arlene accused him of stealing money from her purse. He was adjudicated a JD (juvenile delinquent) and sent to an upstate New York detention facility. Less than a year later Wade returned even angrier; he quit school and, like Joel, bummed around.

Belynda was determined to earn her diploma. That one accomplishment would set her apart from her family.

She made arrangements for Mr. Nokar to tutor her in English and math at home. Another favorite teacher, Mr. Canton,* tutored her in history and science. They believed in her, kept up her morale. When, in mid-May, she donned her cap and gown and received her diploma along with her classmates, Belynda felt, for the first time in her life, a sense of accomplishment and self respect.

On May 28, 1968, Belynda gave birth to her first child, a girl she named Lori Marena.* A few days later, Kay, who had since married, would give birth to her first child, also a girl, on July 1.

The day following Lori's delivery, Belynda and the baby accompanied her uncle Johnny Luke and Kate to Tryon, North Carolina, where her father, Tommy Lee Kirby, was living.

Belynda had known since she was sixteen that her father was still alive, drunk most of the time, and living down the road from Clara in Georgia. "Tommy dead?" Clara told her niece, when she learned Arlene said he had died. "Your mamma knows good and well he ain't dead."

Tommy had since moved to Tryon, a remote rural town. Belynda had not seen her father since she was ten, but if she ever needed him, it was now. She had no one else.

Deep in the Blue Ridge mountains of North Carolina in the late 1960s, the pin-dot town of Tryon boasted a backwoods citizenry of fewer than one thousand, a post office, small market, hardware store, and gas station. Tommy Kirby was working in a yarn mill that employed many of Tryon's residents, and he was trying to stay sober. His live-in girlfriend had departed shortly before Belynda's arrival, but the ranch-style house still evidenced a woman's care; it was relatively clean. Compared to the hovel in which Tommy's mother resided, the house was a castle.

Maude Kirby Rogers* had relocated from Rossville to the Carolina hills, but her lodgings were more reminiscent of her hillbilly childhood in Sparta, Tennessee. She rarely swept her floors, and assorted junk spilled from her shack into the yard. Goats leisurely poked around in the debris, both inside and out. Belynda instructed Maude that Lori was to be tended to only in Tommy's house.

Maude delighted in her little great-granddaughter. She was sixty-seven years old and had lived a hard life, but every day she pushed the stroller the five miles to town and the five miles back, her head held high as a queen's. Belynda found work at the yarn factory and settled in to raise Lori. She was determined to give her daughter the closeness and security she herself had never had.

The calm in the Kirby household lasted three months. One evening, at about two in the morning, Belynda heard her father pull up. He was with another man, and they were laughing loudly. She knew by the sound of their voices that they had been drinking. Belynda quickly slipped on her robe, checked on Lori, who was sleeping soundly in her crib, then answered the door. The men stumbled in.

Tommy swung open the refrigerator and handed his friend a beer. The men sat at the kitchen table eyeing Belynda.

"So, Tommy, this is your daughter," his buddy said.

Belynda looked at the bald, fat man staring at her. She tightened the belt of her robe. "Just a minute," she said and walked back into her bedroom. She could hear the men laughing. Then she returned to the kitchen.

Tommy leaped to his feet. "Belynda, hey, hold it! Calm down! Calm down!"

The .38 snub-nose was pointed directly at him.

"Tell your friend to get up off that chair and get out of the house." Belynda's voice was level. "Both of you. Get out."

The men stumbled out to Tommy's car. The engine rumbled and the tires squealed down the dirt driveway. Tommy did not return that night. The following evening he was sullen but repentant. They lived an uneasy truce.

Several weeks later Maude Kirby fell off a chair in her house and broke her neck; she subsequently died. Stranded, with no one to care for her infant, Belynda called her mother. Would she help out with Lori for a while? Belynda needed to get on her feet financially. Arlene agreed. She and Rosalind drove down to Tryon and the home of her newly resurrected husband.

Arlene returned with Lori to Holtsville, Long Island, where she was living with Frank McDonald. Three months later, Arlene had not returned Lori. She told Belynda she had no time to make the drive. The baby stayed with her grandmother for six months.

Why would Belynda have entrusted her daughter to a woman whose behavior had so terrified her? Belynda saw her decision as a practical one: she thought she had no other choice. Her cousin Kay took a different view. "Belynda came down to North Carolina and things didn't work out the way she thought. She thought for once in her life she was going to have a father, some security, and there she was wrong again. Belynda was starved for love, affection. She was afraid of Arlene, but she was like a little puppy looking for a pat. Maybe she thought this being Arlene's first grandchild, it would turn her around. Maybe she was hoping her mother would change."

By 1968, Arlene appeared to have found relative stability in a relationship and a promising new business. Frank McDonald, who at thirty-seven was three years Arlene's junior, was an affable man whose "live and let live" philosophy had carried him through his wife's death from cancer and the subsequent separation from his three young children. He was lonely and, like Bob Lotz, attended Parents without Partners meetings. There he met Arlene Kirby Lotz.

Arlene told McDonald that her first husband

was dead. She said she had recently divorced her second, an abusive alcoholic who was a deputy sheriff. Lotz, she said, was stalking her, and she had taken a few "pops" at him with her gun.

McDonald was impressed with Arlene's strong will and glamorous looks. She was intelligent, had a head for business. And she was fascinated by the workings of his trucking company.

During the next two years, as they lived and worked together, Frank would see quite a different side of Arlene Kirby Lotz. He would come to understand that she and her children were bound for self-destruction.

Chapter Twelve

In 1968, Arlene moved her sons and four-year-old daughter into Frank McDonald's Commack residence. Frank impressed her as a person of strong personal character. He had goals for himself. In her recollection, he was working for the post office when they met, but he dreamed of becoming an entrepreneur. He was constantly talking about wanting his own business. Finally, one evening, she told him, "If you want this bad enough, you will get it, and the time has come: Put up or shut up." He looked at her kind of funny and the McDonald grin came over his face and he said, "You know, you're right." She was named vice president of the operation. This, in Arlene's memory, was the birth of Five Star Trucking and her role in its development.

The company had, in fact, long been in existence when McDonald met Arlene. At its inception in the early 1960s, Frank and his partner

Lou Day* were doing business as Data Delivery. By the time he began dating Arlene he was ready to incorporate, but that decision, Frank recalls, "wasn't on account of her at all. We needed to dig up three people for incorporation purposes only. We all had magnificent titles but we were only truck drivers." Arlene, McDonald, and Day drew moderate salaries and often worked twenty-hour days driving any one of the fleet of Mercedes trucks on mail routes for paper-product companies and clothing stores, among them A&S department store.

Arlene remembered her years with McDonald and Five Star as a happy period. Frank was a friend, a thoughtful person. When he paid you a compliment he meant it, and he could give you constructive criticism without hurting your feelings. McDonald valued her self-reliance, while all her partners had seen her independence as "a thorn in their side." And he was not jealous of her relationship with her children, which Arlene described as "one of trust in one another."

Arlene was pleased that her sons were coming into their own during their teen years in Commack. "They were participating in everyday activities where young adults were concerned, with a working mother. They were striving for more and more independence, and that was no problem for me because, after all, they were becoming

Bob Caris. Southampton, 1984. (*Arlene Caris*)

Arlene Caris in Bedford Prison, 1992. She claimed she killed her husband after enduring years of abuse. (*Arlene Caris*)

Belynda, age 4; Wade, age 1; Arlene; and Joel, age 3 in 1953. (*Tom Kirby*)

Arlene Kirby,
Jacksonville,
Florida, 1958.

Tommy Lee Kirby,
Broadchannel,
New York, 1956.
(*Arlene Caris*)

The Kirby trailer in Riverhead, New York. (*Arlene Caris*)

Joel, age 6;
Belynda, age 7;
and Wade, age 4, on
Christmas, 1955.
(*Arlene Caris*)

Arlene Kirby in a
neck brace after an
accident in 1960.

40 Adams Lane, Southampton, New York. The house
has since been demolished.

Bob and Arlene Caris
on their wedding day
in Southampton,
June 19, 1971.
(*Clifford Cox*)

Bob and Arlene on
their wedding day
with Rosalind, 1971.

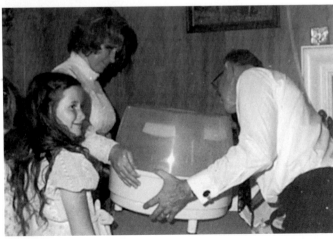

Arlene with Belynda on Belynda's wedding day,
December 7, 1974. (*Bob Caris*)

Belynda and Fred Sablonski's wedding in Southampton,
1974. From left to right: Arlene, Fred, Belynda, Bob.

Belynda with Kay Waldrop in 1994. (*Charles Waldrop*)

Loretta "Lori" Kathran Coco, May 1986, Southampton High School Graduation.

SharonWheeler, Bob Caris's daughter, and her son, Josh, 21, in April 1995. (*Ron Kirkland*)

Detective Fred Nordt of the
Southampton Police Dept.
(*Russ Ditsler*)

Senior Investigator Don
Delaney of the New York
State Police Major Case
Squad. (*Courtesy Suffolk
County Homicide Dept.*)

Senior Investigator Steve Oates, supervisor with the
New York State Police, and Captain William Heesch.
(*Courtesy Suffolk County Homicide Dept.*)

Belynda and Fred Sablonski, 1995. (*Kay Waldrop*)

Wade Kirby in a mug shot taken in 1984, after his arrest for rape in Medford, Long Island. (*Courtesy Suffolk County Police Dept.*)

Rosalind with daughter Conchetta and husband, Tony, at Denamora Prison. (*Courtesy Denamora Prison*)

young men. They were not kids. They were big boys, so I expected them to start showing some signs of growing up and having lives of their own."

Frank McDonald's view of the boys was radically different. From the start he saw Wade Kirby as "walking trouble. You'd look him right in the eye, and you could tell he wasn't all there mentally. Kind of crazy. The guy was very unpredictable, a cutup, a wise guy."

McDonald described Joel as a smooth operator, always looking for some easy-money scam. "Joel was slicker than Wade. He thought he was real smart, but fact was, you could trip Joel up real easy-like." Like the time Joel ripped off Five Star, expecting to have struck gold.

Joel was seventeen when he began driving for Five Star. One of his assignments was to deliver a truckload of boxes marked "medical supplies" to the Brooklyn docks. From there the merchandise would be shipped to a South American drug company. Joel's truck never reached the pier. "Joel thought it was drugs so he ended up stealing the entire shipment," McDonald later recalled. "It wasn't drugs. It was only metric scales. He thought he was getting away with something, but he got away with nothing."

McDonald contacted the FBI, which confirmed that Joel Kirby had indeed stolen the shipment. Kirby was sent to a federal detention facility in Manhattan. The FBI did not prosecute, and McDonald did not press charges.

When the boys were at home together they fought, "not knock-down-drag-out fights, but those kids were emotionally disturbed. They were bed wetters up through their teens." Arlene told Frank that Belynda's husband had been killed in Vietnam. Belynda had, Arlene said, used her husband's life insurance money to purchase a home in North Carolina.

In the fall of 1968, Belynda returned to reclaim her baby, Lori, and temporarily joined the extended McDonald/Kirby household. She and her mother were often at odds. Arlene complained to McDonald about Belynda's promiscuity, her "laying down her own colorful little career. Belynda was fast earning her little reputation of promiscuity unbeknownst to me. My daughter was a very promiscuous young woman. Everybody in town knew about it, but me."

Belynda, however, recalls only a grueling work schedule that at least enabled her to rent a small apartment and hire a baby-sitter for Lori. "My mother called me a tramp, but there were only three men in my life until I got married to Paul [Dubin]. I thought I was in love with them all."

In McDonald's eyes, Belynda was a troubled young woman still searching for her mother's love and acceptance. It was clear to Frank that the girl did not know what she wanted. Part of her confusion was, he felt, rooted in her inability to stand up to her powerful mother. Admittedly, Arlene was a strong woman. Belynda's sudden marriage to Paul Dubin was, McDonald believed, "a way to get away from her mother. She barely knew the guy and she's running off to get married." Frank had a bad feeling about that whirlwind romance.

Like Belynda, Joel had been looking to escape his domineering mother. He found such an "out" in early 1968 when he joined the Navy. The young man whom Belynda would describe as her "knight in shining armor" was Joel's Navy drinking buddy. Paul Dubin and Joel had formed a fast friendship off base, drinking and locked in the brig for fighting and drunken disorder. Joel had shown Paul a picture of his pretty blond sister and told him their mother was going to make "big bucks" in a trucking business.

Belynda's daughter, Lori, was about fourteen months old when she began receiving letters from Dubin. She had not dated since Marena, and she found Paul a charming correspondent. She fell in love with his letters. Love letters. The kind of poetry over which romance-novel heroines languish. After Paul's second letter, she gave him her phone number. His voice, a lush Southern drawl, was slow and easy. He wrote about his feelings, his dreams, his Cajun homeland on the Louisiana bayou. "This guy," she thought, "had Prince Charming written all over him." She did not know he was writing from jail.

When Belynda finally met the tall, dark-haired, blue-eyed Dubin in December 1969, she thought: "He's the answer to everything I've ever been looking for." They married on January 12, 1970, thirty-two days after they first met. Belynda was twenty, Dubin twenty-one. He took her home to New Iberia, a coastal town in southern Louisiana known for its swamps and its Tabasco sauce.

Iberia was one of the last territories in Louisiana to be colonized by French explorers, largely because of its man-eating natives. On April 9, 1682, an expedition led by René-Robert Cavelier La Salle claimed the country through which the Mississippi River flowed and all the land it drained as belonging to King Louis XIV. But Iberia would not be settled until the mid-1700s when a few French trappers and smugglers braved the cannibalistic Attakapas tribes. The homes of these early settlers were built of the most abundant materials in "New Iberia": virgin trees, loamy soil and water, and green moss.

It was the moss, abundant and tenacious, that

formed Belynda's initial impression of New Iberia. Spanish moss, heavy, clinging to the trees, weighted down in the muggy swamp air. The moss seemed to be everywhere. It made her skin crawl, made her feel like crying.

If Belynda experienced any relief escaping her mother, it was short-lived. In Paul's mother, Lyla Dubin,* Belynda found Arlene's Cajun counterpart. "Lyla was Louisiana coon ass, true French Cajun. Very down-home. Very domineering. Lyla didn't take any crap from anybody. She told everyone what to do."

Lyla was a gambler who ran bouree games. Bouree is not for the meek at heart. Bouree gambling in Bayou country means high stakes, hard liquor, fistfights, and guns. Lyla also worked part-time for the sheriff's department, a job that was convenient in view of her son's frequent arrests for drunken brawling. During Paul's sojourns drying out at the New Iberia jailhouse, Lyla brought him home-cooked meals, cigarettes, and magazines. Paul's father was less tolerant of his son's antics. A good-looking man with thick white hair, Ken Dubin* worked the offshore oil rigs and did his best to ignore the respective addictions of his wife and son.

Belynda chronicled the demise of her relationship with Dubin, "From the time the ring went on my finger, that's when Dr. Jekyll turned into

Mr. Hyde." Remarkably, although not surprisingly, Belynda's marriage to Paul mirrored her mother's to Tommy Kirby. Paul Dubin's job offshore working the oil fields kept him away from home for seven-day stretches every other week, and Belynda was left in their large apartment with her two-year-old. She had no friends apart from Dubin's cousin Cathy.

The young couple had been married two weeks when Paul returned home, set down his duffel bag, showered, slipped on his high school ring, and left to go out with his friends. Belynda found his wedding ring on the bathroom sink. She spent the night crying at Cathy's house. Dubin found her there, three days later. He was apologetic, and Belynda was anxious to forgive him.

But Paul continued carousing with his friends and left his wife alone. He didn't want to introduce Belynda to any of his buddies. And when he was home she couldn't even go to the supermarket or the mailbox unless he accompanied her. He was obsessively possessive.

They had been married about a month when one night as he was leaving she barred the door with her body. "You're not taking my car and going out with your friends and leaving me sitting home by myself." Belynda told him. "I'm not putting up with this anymore!"

His first punch knocked her across the room.

Then he flung himself at her and kept on punching. She quit making any noise and lay there on the floor. By the time he left that night, her mouth was a bloody mess.

She told herself, If I'm gonna make this work, I shouldn't fight with him. I shouldn't fight back. Don't say anything, don't do anything.

But he would pluck every single nerve fiber she had.

Several months later, while Paul was away on his offshore shift, a tall thin man wearing a suit came to the door. He identified himself as an FBI agent. Belynda's legs felt like water as she watched him take a seat in her sparsely furnished living room. He began asking her questions about her brother Joel. Had she seen him recently? Belynda shook her head. Had Joel called? No. The agent did not offer any information about what Joel had done, and Belynda was too frightened to ask. She had enough to deal with. She had just learned that she was pregnant again.

With Belynda married, Joel in the Navy, and Wade in Tennessee working, Arlene told Frank McDonald, as a chef, only she and Rosalind remained in the McDonald home. Frank began to see subtle changes in his relationship with his fiancée in the summer of 1970. Only months before, Arlene had seemed delighted with her engagement ring and the admiring comments it elicited. Arlene loved the adulation. She smiled, reveling in the envious stares. McDonald knew she had no intention of disclosing to anyone, not even to Rosalind, that her "diamond" was only glass.

Lately, though, she was drifting away from him. The affectionate, almost ingratiating woman he had fallen in love with had become cold and withdrawn. She told him she wanted to spend more time with Bob Lotz's stepson and his wife, who ran a Carvel ice cream stand on eastern Long Island. When McDonald asked Arlene about those visits, she was very secretive. Then the stories she told him about her past kept changing. He prided himself on his excellent memory, and he knew something was just not jibing. Like the time she told him she had been abused, then said she had "beat the hell out of Tommy Kirby," her first husband. She told him she put bars of soap in a sock, tied the top, and worked the guy over. McDonald sensed that Arlene had enjoyed those brutal episodes; he could not picture her as an abused wife.

In the spring, McDonald went to Ohio to visit his three children. Since his wife's death, they were being raised by his mother-in-law. Arlene had said she would visit Bob Lotz's stepson, one of her usual trips. Frank phoned the couple whose number Arlene had left; she was not there. No, they did not know where Arlene was. They had not seen or heard from Arlene Lotz in years.

Frank did not know what to believe: what had his fiancée told him that was true, what was fabrication? Which were the diamonds, which were glass? Did she even know the difference? He felt distinctly uncomfortable.

Neither Frank McDonald nor Bob Caris, whom Arlene had begun dating, knew that the woman they both loved was leading a double life. Frank would not learn of Caris's existence until Arlene announced her engagement to him. Caris would never know that during their courtship his fiancée had been living under another man's roof, constructing yet another life for herself in a tenuous, dangerous game.

PART FOUR

Chapter Thirteen

The deserts of Saudi Arabia have been described alternately as brutal and poetic. Sudden hundred-mile-an-hour windstorms fling dust and stones like shrapnel. It may not rain for years; then, without warning, the earth is violently deluged. Vast yellow dunes and black shale outcrops are said to harbor evil spirits. Summer temperatures hover at 160 degrees under a sizzling white marble sky, 120 degrees in the occasional shade. Winter starscapes above the cool sands are achingly beautiful.

In the town of Dhahran on the Persian Gulf, men gather in open squares to drink sweet tea from silver flasks. Women draped in black veils drift among spice and bread stalls in the *souq,* market. Thieves caught stealing have their hands chopped off. The punishment for murder, rape, or proven adultery is death, execution-style, in the street, whether the offender is a nomad or a royal.

On a hilltop in Dhahran near Well No. 7, the Arabian American Oil Company, known as Aramco, built its employee compound. If Norman Rockwell had painted a *Saturday Evening Post* cover of a 1950s American suburb, it would have resembled this transplanted community in the Sahara. Aramco's employees lived in prim white clapboard houses, many with wraparound porches and red pitched roofs, or, like the Caris family, in California ranch-style homes. There were tennis courts, a beauty salon, a bowling alley, a swimming pool, soda fountains, a baseball diamond, and a movie house that showed films three times a week. The supermarket stocked familiar brands.

Life in this sheltered enclave was orderly and insulated. Only scattered palm trees and irrigation streams that fed small home gardens betrayed the desert siting of Aramco's compound.

One of Sharon Caris Wheeler's earliest memories was of her father telling her that he would be going away for a while. At the time she was six, and they were living in Whitestone, a semi-suburb of Manhattan. One Sunday morning, her father put his newspaper aside and explained that he would be leaving soon for Saudi Arabia, a place that was far away. He would work there for an oil company, but in two years she and her mother would join him.

To young Sharon, two years might as well have been a lifetime. Her father was the center of her universe. The hours they spent together every Sunday reading aloud from the funny papers enabled her to learn to read at an early age. She was something of a tomboy and on weekends the two of them would go fishing or fly the model airplanes he built or tinker with his model railroad. Dad was a softy when it came to discipline. "Oh, Sharon just wasn't thinking," he would tell his wife, Sally, when she had done something wrong. And, of course, whatever offense Sharon had committed, she never repeated. She did not want to disappoint her dad.

Soon letters and photographs began arriving from Saudi Arabia. Ten-page typed letters, single-spaced, came like clockwork every week, "letters by the ton," she would call them. Sharon and her mother joined Bob Caris when she was eight, but the letter-writing tradition established between father and daughter would continue for more than thirty years.

In the early 1950s the oil conglomerate Aramco, which had been a joint venture between Esso and Mobil, afforded a luxurious lifestyle abroad for its expatriates. Every two years, the company picked up the tab for its employees' three-month vacations—anywhere in the world. All the families had servants, but since Arab women were, by Saudi law, not permitted within the complex on the hill, household help was male. The Caris family had a gardener, a chef, a cleaning man, and an ironing boy. But, seven times a day the Saudis would take out their prayer rugs and Korans, and the Caris household, along with the rest of the kingdom, literally came to a halt. At dusk, the natives left the fenced-in community; only the Americans and a handful of Dutch remained.

Within Aramco's cloister, traditional American values prevailed. Neighbors gathered for barbecues. A bright-yellow school bus took the children to in-camp American school, which Sharon attended until she was twelve. The Fiesta room of the communal dining hall, frequented by the single men, featured thick milk shakes and hamburgers.

"The way you live now, Sharon, is what I've provided for you," Bob Caris told his daughter, "but the way you'll live the rest of your life depends on how you're going to provide for yourself."

Education, Caris believed, was the key to success. Sharon left Dhahran to attend an American high school for embassy children in Beirut, Lebanon, where she excelled in academics and was also a cheerleader. Aramco paid her airfare back to Saudi Arabia for all holidays and for summer vacation.

Sharon spent her junior year at the American Community School, a boarding school in Lugano, Switzerland, founded by prominent New York socialite Mary Crisp Fleming. The stunning historic villa catered to children of very wealthy families from the Philadelphia Main Line, Chestnut Hill in Boston, and Dallas and Fort Worth oil dynasties. Girls wore full-length mink coats to tea. During the winter they went skiing in St. Moritz, and they took regular excursions to La Scala for the Italian opera season. Classes, taught in French, instructed the girls on the requisite social graces for ambassador's wives. Every three weeks, a ball was held at the villa or one of its sister French and Italian boarding schools. Dress was formal, long white opera gloves de rigeur.

By the time Sharon returned to the States to attend college, she had had a cosmopolitan education and seen much of the world.

To Robert Caris, a former Pan American pilot and radio operator and an avid gourmet, such security and luxury was appealing but not extraordinary. The Carises were a Main Line family from Pennsylvania; its patriarch, Ivan Caris, was an executive at a leading New York insurance company. Sharon thought of her grandparents as very proper English. "You always had to wear white gloves and no matter how thin you were, you were to wear a girdle so that your rear end was not attracting anyone."

The soft-spoken, quietly dignified Caris married a genteel woman from New Jersey, whom he met while on a flying assignment in Florida. Sally was a gourmet cook and an amateur fashion designer, and, like Bob, she enjoyed traveling.

For Sharon, who had been adopted by the Carises as an infant, growing up within Aramco's complex was a "great life." But the insular community was confining to many residents. Drinking was prohibited among the native Muslim population, but in-camp alcoholism became a problem. Caris, though, was health-conscious and kept himself trim largely by avoiding alcohol. Ironically, he smoked incessantly, as many as four or five packs a night when he worked long stretches as a radio operator, directing plane and oil tanker activity. On social occasions he had a beer or two. Sharon recalled, "The biggest thrill of Dad's life was to come back to the U.S. and have a Guinness stout."

By 1964, Sharon had graduated with a degree in psychology from Whittier, an expensive private college in Southern California, married classmate James Wheeler and had her first child, a son they named William. The Wheelers settled in Northern California. Her father's letters still arrived like clockwork, seven to ten typed pages; nothing new, just keeping in touch. But when Sally's health started failing the Carises decided to retire back to the States.

Between his nontaxable income with Aramco, a fifty-thousand-dollar-a-year living stipend, and a hefty investment portfolio, Caris had amassed, over a thirty-year period, a substantial nest egg. "He was," Sharon said, "very rich."

When the couple returned to America in mid-1964, they chose the upscale community of Southampton on the shores of the Atlantic. They felt quite at home among its affluent, conservative residents.

The house at 40 Adams Lane was modest, too modest for Sally Caris. Bob told his wife that they would be traveling most of the time. But Sally's health worsened, and when it became clear that they would do little traveling, Caris took a job at ITT as a ship-to-shore radio operator. He had long been a ham radio buff and had developed a worldwide network of amateur broadcasters. It was through this network that he first made contact with an ITT radio operator, Marvin Fields.* Caris told Fields that he was interested in working in Southampton as a ship-to-shore operator. The radio job at the coastal station appealed to him. It would keep him active and involved with people.

When Caris joined ITT in 1967, he and Fields struck up an immediate friendship. "Bob got along with everybody," Fields said. Sally Caris was "a dainty, quiet, gentle woman," and like Fields's wife, an excellent cook and housekeeper; the Caris home was always immaculate. The couple were very attentive to each other, and Fields often heard Caris affectionately call his wife "Dear."

Bob Caris seemed to be a very gentle fellow, very much a family man.

In 1969, Sally Caris died. A family man without a family, Bob Caris was adrift. His letters to his daughter reflected his loneliness. Sharon encouraged him to come to California for a visit, but he said he could not leave his job. A methodical man, Caris found solace in his routine.

Sharon hoped her father would meet a woman who would appreciate his patience and kind heart. She worried, though. Bob Caris was, for all his travels and education, not a worldly man. He was, Sharon knew, very naive.

In the summer of 1970, the tone of Bob Caris's letters to his daughter changed. For the first time since his wife's death, he sounded optimistic about life. He had met a woman, he wrote. She had a young daughter. He seemed quite taken with both of them, especially the little girl. Her name was Rosalind and she was eight, the same age as Sharon's oldest son.

Soon her father was making plans. "I'm going to be happy again," he wrote. "I'm going to have my old life back."

Chapter Fourteen

The little girl who so enchanted Bob Caris showed a very different face to her immediate family. Young Rosalind reminded Arlene's sister Clara of a "striped snake, the kind we was always told as a kid was really mean. Mean and sneaky and lying. That girl was the most hateful thing I'd ever seen." Clara warned Arlene, "If you don't start correcting that one she's going to be the death of you."

Willie May, too, saw Rosalind as destructive. "Rosalind was jealous of anyone giving her mother affection. That child was going to undo that marriage."

But as far as Arlene was concerned, Rosalind could do no wrong.

By the time Arlene met Bob Caris, pretty eight-year-old Rosalind Lotz already had a repertoire of experiences quite foreign to those of the mild-mannered widower. The Lotz household into which Rosalind had been born had, admittedly, not been a tranquil one, and the daily violence had made its impression on the child. Physical fights between her parents were routine. A devoted daughter, Rosalind invariably came to her mother's aid.

When Rosalind was three she intervened between her parents as they fought outside their Lake Ronkonkoma home, with dire consequences. Lotz and Arlene were talking quietly in the backyard when suddenly he started slapping her. Rosalind later would recall, "When the cops came they saw blood coming out of my mouth, and they thought that he hit me. No, they had to pry my jaw open to get his flesh out. He went to his grave missing a chunk of his calf because I took it out."

In Rosalind's eyes Belynda, too, was an adversary. Their shared birthday was a brutal coincidence in a household where attention was at a premium. She particularly resented what seemed to her to be Belynda's independence with the money she earned. Roz expressed her rivalry with a vengeance.

Shortly before Lori was born, teenage Belynda bought two goldfish. One was gold, the other black. Fancy goldfish in a costly bowl purchased with money she earned from a department store job. The fish were the only pets allowed in the

Lotz household. Belynda kept them atop the living room television, where it was warm, and she cared for them lovingly. One evening she returned home and, as usual, checked on the fish. What she saw made her reel. Two fish heads were floating, disembodied, in the bowl. Rosalind stood beside her sister, smiling. She told Belynda that she had bitten off their tails and eaten them. She said she was angry at not being allowed to feed the fish. Roz was then four years old. "I'm the original sushi girl," she said years later.

In that hair-trigger volatility Rosalind took after her mother. Arlene seemed to be a magnet for violence. It held for her, Rosalind believed, an eerie fascination. "It was like Mom was addicted to fighting."

There was always a sense of the unknown, a darkness that at any moment could engulf Arlene and would swallow them all whole.

Early on, the little girl learned how to avoid her mother's wrath. She was schooled by her brothers, who had their own battle scars. If Mom came in the driveway fast, if you saw the car jerk to a stop, you knew she was in one of her moods. On those days "Mom really got carried away. Flesh on flesh, object on flesh. It was like she got a rush from it."

Joel would cover his face with his hands and

cry, but Wade broke away and ran. Arlene would chase after him in the car and drag him back home screaming.

In Rosalind's eyes, Joel was "the softy, a sweetheart, any woman's dream." A nature and animal lover, he seemed to her to be a real gentleman. "Joel had a big heart. He would bend over backwards for you."

But Wade, he was like the song "Freebird." Wade was a heartbreaker. He was not the kind to settle down. He loved his motorcycles, the wind in his hair. If a girl got too serious, he would tell Roz to give her a message: "Tell her I had a good time, but it's over."

Rosalind loved Joel, but she idolized Wade. Wade was the outlaw. He was rough, always in trouble. Still, she wanted only to be near him, and he knew it. Even at a young age Wade could read women, their desires, their vulnerabilities. Sometimes he took her along when he had a date. The three of them—Wade, his girl, and his kid sister—would go to the beach or to a drive-in. Wade's girlfriends were impressed. How many guys would take their little sister out on a date? How sweet.

As Rosalind got older she knew her brother was using her. But she didn't care. Wade was her hero. "Wade was Jesse James. He was just born in the wrong century."

* * *

In the summer of 1970 Wade Kirby was making his own modern-day history. While Bob Caris was wooing Arlene, eighteen-year-old Wade was visiting his uncle, Ray Kirby, in Chattanooga, Tennessee. He had gone to Byron, Georgia, in early July for the Atlanta International Pop Festival, then returned to the downtown boardinghouse where Ray lived. The house was owned by Ella Hall.

Shortly before ten a.m. on August 3, the body of sixty-one-year-old Ella Hall was discovered at the foot of her bed, a pillowcase wrapped around her neck. Her apartment had been ransacked, and a pistol she owned was missing. Robbery was considered the motive in the killing.

Reports placed Wade and his uncle in the company of Mrs. Hall the previous evening. Their landlady, said some, had a habit of seducing her young male tenants, Wade Kirby among them. Others said she had angered Ray Kirby by rebuffing his unwanted advances. Both Kirbys were interviewed, then released. Wade headed for his cousin Kay's trailer in Fort Ogelthorpe, Georgia, where she was living with her truckdriver husband, Charlie, and her two daughters.

Kay was surprised and delighted at the unexpected visit. Wade played with her little girl, Sharon, "like everything was just fine. Nothing different about him, he was just the same old Wade, good-looking, joking, coming and going." When her mother, Clara, sent her a copy of the August 7 *Chattanooga Times*, Kay was stunned.

The headline read: "Hippie Charged in Murder."

A transient 18-year-old youth from New York has been charged with the Tuesday morning strangulation of a Highland Park woman. . . . Wade Frederick Kirby was arrested in front of 1506 S. Willow Street by Officer Jesse Harrell. The address was the home of the victim, Mrs. Ella Hall.

A photo of Wade Kirby, spread-eagled and restrained by two detectives, accompanied the article.

The following day the murder story had been moved from page three to the front page: "New York Youth Says Drank Beer, 'Freaked Out' before Woman Slain." The front-page photo was captioned, "Suspect Arrested: The New York youth momentarily broke loose from detectives and lunged at the photographer shouting, 'If you take my picture I'll kill you.'"

Arlene was convinced that her "happy-go-lucky" son had been wrongly accused; the real culprit was his uncle Charles Ray. She had warned both her boys to stay away from Tommy Lee Kirby's family; they were trouble. Especially illiterate Ray, who, like other members of Tommy's family, "had some screws loose."

About five months before Hall's murder, Arlene had had a dire premonition. As she later recalled, "It wasn't a dream. I was wide awake. I saw this room, apartment, with one bed and a little living area. By a table I saw two chairs. I saw a sitting figure. I couldn't tell if it was Wade or his brother. All I saw was my son's head down on the table, as though he was asleep or passed out. I saw Charles Ray come in the door, reach over and slip a pillowcase around the woman's neck and throttle her. He shook her, threw her on the floor and spit on her face. It was Ray who did it." But Wade, not Ray, was charged.

Bob Caris's daughter, Sharon Wheeler, would later claim that her father knew nothing about Wade's criminal past. But Arlene insists that she told her fiancé all. "I didn't pull any punches. Bob seemed supportive of me. He stated he didn't know how he would handle something like that. I told him there's only one way to handle this: 'He's got to have a decent attorney.'"

Wade pled guilty to involuntary manslaughter and was remanded to the Chattanooga jail, where he served another year.

* * *

In early February 1971, Bob Caris, Arlene, and Rosalind drove to Melbourne, Florida, where Belynda was living. Paul Dubin's parents had moved from New Iberia, and their devoted son followed. Belynda was nearly nine months pregnant, due any day. Bob Caris impressed Belynda as a shy man, refined, well educated, intelligent, quiet. Her mother was on her guard; polite and low-key, dressed very well—as was Rosalind. They all seemed to be having an enjoyable vacation. Arlene was spending money like it was water.

Perhaps Mom had found what she was looking for, Belynda thought. She seemed at peace with the world. The anger wasn't there. You could breathe around her. You didn't have to walk on tiptoe.

On February 17, Belynda began having contractions. Bob Caris drove her to the hospital, where she delivered her second daughter, Monica.

Several days later, Sharon received a letter from her father. "Arlene and I took a trip to Florida," he wrote. "But don't worry, Sharon. We slept in separate rooms."

Sharon shook her head. Dad was such a square.

In the spring of 1971, Arlene Kirby obtained a divorce from her first and only husband, Tommy Lee Kirby. She and Bob Caris were married on June 19, 1971, in a quiet ceremony at 40 Adams Lane.

Belynda, who was living in Florida, did not attend the wedding. Neither did Joel, who, as Arlene later recalled, was "off bumming around." Having served less than two years on involuntary manslaughter, Wade had been released from jail in time for the wedding. Arlene's two "love children," Wade and Rosalind, stood side by side as their mother took her vows. Arlene wore white.

Bob Caris's coworkers at WSL, the ITT ship-to-shore station, called her "Wonder Woman." There was nothing his new wife could not do. She drove ten-ton trucks, learned welding—Bob bought her a welding outfit for Christmas—and she could certainly take care of herself in a jam. Early in the marriage, Caris recounted to his friend Marvin Fields just how self-assured his new wife was. They had gone on a shopping trip to New York and parked in a garage. When they returned, someone was in the process of stealing the car radio. Arlene didn't waste any time with that guy, Fields recalled Caris saying, "She beat him up. She threw him out of the car and drove off."

Somebody else might have been intimidated. Not Arlene. She was very aggressive and her husband seemed in awe of her.

Arlene's assertiveness was undoubtedly a relief

to Caris, who had spent the last years of his marriage tending to an ill wife. Still, he was protective. He told Fields about a conversation he and Arlene had had concerning the value of his rather expensive ham radio setup. "In case something happens to me," Bob told his wife, "you should know its real worth."

"I won't sell it," Arlene told him. "I'll get a license and use it myself." Arlene was, Fields believed, capable of doing anything, and she made a point of flaunting her competency.

Mrs. Caris's talents were not limited to the technical crafts. She told her husband of a miracle she had performed. He, in turn, conveyed that incident to his ITT colleagues. Arlene had taken a correspondence course in home aide nursing, sufficient to obtain certification. Subsequently, she had been hired as a day nurse for a man who was paralyzed, and she apparently discovered that she was meant to cure him. While giving him some sort of therapy, she took his neck and twisted it a certain way, and soon after he could walk with a cane. Arlene told her patient's doctor, "He's walking, and you had told him he never would. Now get out of here." The doctor was angry. He said she could have killed him.

Bob seemed bewildered at the physician's response. After all, he told his friends, "The guy was walking!"

Not everyone was as taken with the new Mrs. Caris. Clifford Cox, who had introduced the two after he met Arlene at an East Northport country club, had since married, and his wife, Jill, was deeply suspicious of the striking redhead.

Cliff had found Arlene Lotz very attractive, "very, very talkative, flamboyant"—but too tall for him. He thought his "Mr. Milquetoast" colleague would find her fun and interesting. She claimed to have done everything, even driven race cars disguising herself as a man. Cox gave Caris her phone number. After their first date, Bob seemed to have a new outlook on life. The sadness of losing his wife was fast disappearing.

It all happened very quickly.

Cliff's wife was convinced that the naive widower did not know anything about the woman he had married. A petite redhead who resembled Shirley MacLaine, Jill Cox was a sharp observer of human nature. She had an almost uncanny ability to sense danger. An American Indian medicine man she had once met told her she had the gift of "mind-walking."

Shortly after the Caris marriage, the Coxes moved from Hampton Bays to the Berkshires, and Arlene offered to help. With her brother Johny Luke's two sons, she drove a truckload of home furnishings to the Coxes' new home. When Charlie returned to the Hamptons to take final inventory, Jill was left alone with Arlene. Jill would later recall her discomfort. "Something was out of kilter with Arlene. She talked too much. She told too many stories. It was like she was on a high, she couldn't stop talking. She talked about a policeman she had been married to, that she came up the cellar steps with a gun after him. He was vicious toward her, physically abusive. She said she wouldn't let anyone push her around again."

Jill was disturbed by Arlene's fluency with weapons and by the chilling look in her eyes when she spoke of guns. After Arlene left, Jill felt an overwhelming sense of urgency; she called her husband.

"Something is very wrong with her," she told Cliff.

"Arlene? What do you mean?"

A phrase Jill's own mother often used came into her mind. "There's something wrong with her head," Jill said. "I'm a little leery of her. Maybe you could say something to Bob."

They debated what Cliff might say. In the end, they decided to let it drop. How do you tell a man that his wife is dangerous?

From the time Arlene met Bob Caris, she had raved to her younger daughter about his house, and after their wedding, Rosalind was delighted to claim her own bedroom, her own bathroom, and the large yard, which she had all to herself. She played with Bob's cats, Casey and Herman, and she was curious about his ham radio in the basement. She was always underfoot. But her stepfather was patient and kind, and Rosalind called him Dad. Best of all, her mother was happy, and her unpredictable rages seemed to have abated.

Arlene was, herself, behaving like a kid. Finally able to satisfy what Rosalind even then called her "champagne taste," she frequented Southampton's tony boutiques and specialty shops, bought clothes, jewelry, and shoes in such quantity that Rosalind would later liken her to Imelda Marcos. There were her weekly Saturday salon appointments, cocktail parties, dinners at fine restaurants, and entertaining at home.

Arlene had attained status in the kind of wealthy community she had long sought.

The marriage seemed to be a comfortable partnership. Arlene and Bob both enjoyed puttering around the house and gardening. He tended the vegetable garden; she, the roses and strawberries. On summer weekends they explored flea markets, Bob discovering odds and ends while Arlene made the larger purchases. She had always had a passion for cars, especially 1960s models, and now she could collect and restore them.

Since they shared checking accounts, Arlene was careful to pay her personal bills before Bob saw them—like the two-thousand-dollar bill one month for clothes. That first year of his marriage, Caris wrote glowing reports to Sharon about his beautiful, independent wife, who knew how to manage money as well as cook. "She stuck to the old-fashioned way: 'The way to a man's heart is through his stomach,'" Rosalind observed. "And he was very particular about his food. The first time she cooked a meal for him, I could tell he was impressed."

Bob was also very particular about orderliness in his house, and Arlene kept up its appearance. On their first anniversary, she told Rosalind that she now owned the house on Adams Lane. Bob had, she said, given her the deed—a gift worth about three hundred fifty thousand dollars.

The impression Bob Caris made on Arlene's Georgia clan was that of a courtly man who deferred to his wife's whims and moods. Their fondness for Caris grew in the subsequent years when the couple, along with Rosalind, visited during the summers. Clara thought Bob Caris was "the sweetest man ever was. Had to be, to put up with her. Never in all them years did that man ever raise his voice to that woman. She talked to him like he was dirt, pure dirt, and the man never batted an eye. She'd tell him, and Bob'd go right along with her, 'Whatever you say.' Never contradicted her about nothing. A fine man."

Still, Clara worried about Rosalind. "That girl's gonna do them both in," she predicted.

In Her Own Words: Arlene Caris

Joel had acute lymphoma, commonly known as Hodgkin's disease, which is cancer of the lymph node. Joel said [to his doctor]: "I want my mom here. I know she understands your medical jargon far better than I do."

I wasn't working as a practical nurse at that time. I started it with a correspondence course, I don't even remember where. I just got the information from some magazine. I was studying at home and to get hands-on experience like with using a lift, and various practices with equipment, and setting up an IV and things like that. I got some by going into the different hospitals and asking to watch, observe, proceedings and wherever I could. I started doing this when I was still working for Macy's. I felt it would be more secure in the future; it would not go out of style.

We had a healthy respect for each other, and

Joel told her [his doctor], "I'm going to be relying a lot on my mother's knowledge and her being able to explain these things to me." But he said, "Just what the hell is lymphoma or Hodgkin's disease?"

She said, "Joel, it is cancer of the lymph nodes and it is inoperable. However, I would like to be wrong about this. I want you in the hospital so tests can be run to determine yes or no."

Bob [Caris] didn't show any concern. He just looked at me as if to say, "Oh, so what," or just sloughed it off as if it was an everyday affair. He didn't even show any concern for my being upset over the fact that my son just may have a terminal illness.

It was '73. I don't know where Belynda was. God only knows where Wade was, because at that particular time he was wandering here, there, wherever the calling was. He'd take a job for whatever they'd hire him, for as long as it put money in his pocket. So he wasn't adverse to getting his hands dirty. That's one thing about both of the boys, they were workers. They were not lazy and they were not dependent on someone else. There was a close tie between them and myself, but after all, I was the only family that they had. Rosalind was always close to both her brothers. Bob showed absolutely no concern, interest, whatever.

It was going downhill even more and more [at home]. I felt that if I included Bob in this consultation where he could see and hear for himself, that at least he would be as well informed as he could be. There were times when he didn't believe that what I was telling him, or that Joel was ill or anything like that. You ever know a person that's pessimistic? And he was the most pessimistic person I have ever known. I felt that the doctors were having problems getting him to speak up and contribute at the consultation. There were a number of times that Joel was hospitalized and I don't know how many times I went up there and dragged Bob with me to visit. I tried to make him feel included, not left out, even after that. For him to think that there wasn't anything wrong with Joel. He said it to me, to hurt me.

For one thing, he was very resentful over the fact that my kids were close to me as they were. He resented that in the worse way. I told him, I said, "There's no point in you resenting them being close to me. Why wouldn't they be? I'm the only family that they have. I worked for them. I provided for them. I couldn't do the impossible and that was be mother and father to them, but I was mother and wage earner and they knew exactly where they stood with me.

There was no doubt about what my position was to them, or vice versa."

They were always there, until they hit the ripe old age of eighteen when they thought they had the world by a tail with a downhill pull, and they were out to do their own thing. All of them, Joel included.

Joel was very, very cooperative right until the end of '77. Finally he told me, he said, "Mother, I know you're not going to like what I'm going to have to say, but this is not living."

He had lost weight. Joel was six two, his normal weight was one hundred and ninety pounds and when he died he weighed less than a hundred pounds. The doctors had said they gave him six months to live. He had told me early in '78, he says, "Mother, I have tried and I've tried and this is not living. It's not worth it to me."

About six weeks before he died, I was by the apartment to see him. We got to talking and he says, "Mother, you know something," he says. "The happiest days of my life was when I was living at home."

He said, those were his very words, "The happiest days of my life were when I was living home."

And I said, "Well, you know, that's kind of—that's an unexpected statement."

He said, "Well, it's the truth. I was happy at home."

I said, "So this big wonderful world was not all that wonderful when you were out there doing your thing?"

He just laughed. He said, "Doing my thing, indeed."

Bob and Belynda, their attitude absolutely stunk. Belynda's attitude toward Joel was so bad that Joel's friend, one of the best friends he had, was so disgusted at Belynda's treatment of Joel that he ordered her out of his house and told her never to set foot at his door again. She was mean to Joel, absolutely mean to him. She showed no compassion whatsoever for him and it made Joel angry.

I got absolutely no support [from Bob]. He would stand and tell me that the world was a better place without my son. Tell me there was nothing wrong with him, that Joel was "just a lazy son of a bitch." How it hurt. The only way I retaliated was to completely ignore him and refuse to say anything about it to him. I just refused to put myself on a lower basis. That takes a hell of a lot of will power. I got to the point where I didn't know what to expect from him and I couldn't care less.

Joel died June 10, 1978. I had him cremated.

He knew he was going to go, and the cremation was his idea. I asked him, "Why?"

And he laughed, he said, "I don't look forward to being food for the worms."

That's the kind of sense of humor he had.

About less than a year before he died, he came up [to the house]. The friend that had brought him there and he walked in on one of Bob's favorite dialogues, and he looked at me and says, "Bob, how long has this been going on?"

Bob was in one of his favorite moods and that was physically or mentally abusing me. Joel walked in on it. Bob said, "None of your damn business."

Joel said, "I'm going to tell you something. My mother is my business. Anything that you do to her you do to me. I never thought that I would live to see the day my mother would take that kind of abuse. She doesn't deserve it. And you know I'll tell you one thing. I better never hear of it happening again or you'll answer to me. I may not be long in this world, but I got news for you, buddy: You better shape up or you sure as hell will answer to me."

So, of course, Bob disappeared to the basement and got on his rig.

Joel said, "Mother, why do you take that from that guy?"

I told him, "Joel, it is not as easy as you'd like

to make it look. I work, I got a home to take care of, I got your sister here that I'm trying to make a halfway decent life for. I'm not getting any younger. An awful lot has to be considered in all ways. The only thing I can do is to place this whole situation in God's hands and trust Him to lead, guide, direct me through it."

Chapter Fifteen

The discovery of Joel's cancer had been, quite literally, by accident. An X-ray taken after he was involved in a car crash showed an abnormality. A biopsy confirmed the clinical diagnosis of Dr. Jane Marion, the family's physician. Joel had asymptomatic Hodgkin's disease, but the prognosis was good if he pursued treatment. He had veterans insurance, so cost was not a factor. But Joel elected not to be compliant. Marion recalled, "He was young. He did not want to be sick. He wanted to do what he wanted to do, and that meant not seeking treatment."

Over the years, Belynda had lost touch with her brothers. Wade, her mother told her, had been "his usual free spirit," traveling and making money when he could as a chef; he was a talented cook as well as a sketch artist. Joel was, for all his intelligence, a laborer. He drove trucks, worked on cars. The solitary occupation suited his nature. He had always been quiet, pensive, always in control of his emotions. He was an observer of life, which he kept at a safe distance.

During the last stages of Joel's illness, Belynda got to know the man her brother had become. A withdrawn and quiet child who had cringed when his mother walked into the room, Joel's escape into the military when he was seventeen had backfired. Navy discipline was not as severe as what he had endured at home, but any form of authority got his hackles up. Once again he was trapped with a taskmaster. He seemed headed for a "BCD"—bad conduct discharge, given the drunken brawls that landed him in the brig with Paul Dubin. But two years after joining the Navy, Joel was released on a medical discharge: he was still a chronic bed wetter. Belynda believed that her brother had simply found another convenient "out" from an oppressive situation. In the subsequent years, Joel lived what Belynda described as a "tumbleweed" life, taking odd jobs that afforded him enough money to travel. But, whereas Wade's escapades were deliberately destructive, Joel's bumming was "more laid-back." By the time Belynda and Fred married, he had settled in North Sea, a community west of Southampton where summer vacationers who could not afford $15,000 a month for oceanfront mansions rented inexpensive bungalows. Joel shared winter rentals with friends, repaired cars, and smoked a good deal of marijuana.

Dr. Marion told Belynda there was every reason to believe that if Joel were compliant—that is, pursued treatment—and had the necessary emotional support, he could recover. The boy was young and otherwise strong. He had an excellent prognosis, but his family's role was especially critical.

Belynda talked with Bob about Joel's illness during their Sunday morning breakfast chats, a tradition begun years before, when she first left Paul Dubin. Bob was sympathetic, supportive of her caring for Joel. Her mother alternated between "playing martyr" and indifference.

Belynda believed that Joel did not comprehend the enormity of his illness. But one thing he knew for sure: he wanted nothing to do with Arlene. He told Belynda he felt worse when he talked to their mother.

For weeks at a time, when he was too sick to care for himself, Joel stayed with the Sabloskis. Belynda drove him to chemotherapy and remained with him as the drugs filled his system, until she could no longer watch him retching in pain. Then she would wait out his sessions in the hallway.

Kay saw her cousin's devotion to Joel as an

attempt to hold on to any remnant of family. "Belynda loved Joel and Joel loved her. He was the last of any connection she felt to her family. She was trying to grab all she could during those last months."

Dr. Marion also observed with interest Belynda's support of Joel's fleeting efforts to help himself recover. The physician could see that his sister had assumed the role of "good mother." Belynda was giving Joel what she so desperately wanted for herself.

As far as Dr. Marion could tell, Belynda was clearly trying to be a good mother to her own daughters. She managed also to keep a sense of humor, despite the brutality of home life. But why had she returned to her mother's home for solace, when Arlene obviously was a distant, if not abusive parent?

Marion believed that Belynda was still trying to win her mother's love and approval. It was, the physician knew, a futile task.

"Your mother is a cancer that needs to be cut out," Marion told Belynda.

During the progression of Joel's illness, Marion also closely observed Arlene. Joel's mother seemed to be totally uninvolved with his treatment. Her lack of interest was striking. "Arlene's attitude was, 'This is something that Joel's gone and done. It's his problem.' "

Marion happened to run into Arlene one evening in a Southampton grocery store. Arlene, who was working as a home health care aide, approached Marion and began talking about the treatment that one of her patients was undergoing. Marion was familiar with that case. She knew the minimal, albeit supportive, role a caregiver could provide. Yet Arlene presented quite an extraordinary picture of herself. Marion later recalled, "You'd think she was Mother Theresa."

What struck Dr. Marion was not only Arlene's grandiosity but the ease with which she told outright lies. Arlene's belief in her own powers was so extreme that the physician sensed a pathology was at work.

Marion knew the importance of trusting both her instinct and her clinical judgment. Trusting her gut reaction had been ingrained in her during her medical studies at Temple University in the 1950s. Her psychiatry mentor had been the esteemed Professor O. Spurgeon English. An author of early textbooks on psychiatry, Professor English advised his students, "Use your intuition. If you sense something is not right, it probably is not."

Marion's intuitive sense was that Joel's mother was a very "malignant personality, someone who touches and destroys with her whole being. Arlene was one of those sweet Southern belles who was dripping, oozing Southern hospitality, someone who was low-class trying to be high-class. There was something not right about her story."

In dealing with Arlene, Jane Marion was reminded of the book *The Bad Seed*. She had seen its Broadway adaptation in 1954 when she was in high school; its plot left a lasting impression of her. The story offered a chilling glimpse into the dark side of a child who committed murder to get what she wanted. Years later in her interactions with the extended Kirby/Caris family, Dr. Marion would ponder the questions posed by that story. What force had caused such people to become what they were? Was it the result of a bad environment? Or was it an inborn, predestined fate that could, at best, be only slightly modified? Marion became intrigued by the psychopathic mind.

Years later she would have the opportunity to observe it close up.

During Joel's illness, Dr. Marion recognized the telltale signs of a personality disorder in Arlene Caris—the narcissistic, grossly inflated view of her self-worth and importance, a truly astounding egocentricity and sense of entitlement. Arlene saw herself as the center of the universe, a superior being who was entitled to live by her own rules. Yet to the casual observer she appeared normal. She was charming, skillful, smart, and very self-confident. Marion sensed that behind Arlene's mask of normalcy lay a dangerously distorted view of the world.

In Dr. Marion's clinical experience, sociopaths or psychopaths were the most difficult patients; they were virtually unresponsive to therapy. "A sociopath has no value system from which to deal, so there is nothing to work with. They simply do not know right from wrong. But they are generally very charming, and when you are with them you love them. It's only after they leave that you realize you've been had."

There was a school of thought that interpreted sociopathy as deriving from a lack of self-esteem. The theory was that sociopaths were fundamentally insecure and overcompensated by inflating themselves to grand proportions. Marion disagreed. To her, sociopaths truly had *superior* self-images and an unwavering belief in that superiority.

Marion was convinced that Arlene utterly believed she was extraordinary. At some point, the woman had crossed the line between truth and lies. Arlene Caris had lost track of where, in fact, that line was.

"You feel sorry for a society that has to deal with someone like that," Marion later explained. "They are very destructive to the nicer part of society, to people who cannot even conceive of that kind of evil. Sociopaths prey on the weak. They destroy, then they pick themselves right up and go on."

For Joel, his mother's pathology could mean the difference between life and death.

The term "sociopath" was not unfamiliar to Belynda. At the time of Joel's diagnosis, she came across an article in *Reader's Digest* on the subject. She read it several times, reviewing repeatedly the points the writer made. Her horror returned to relief. At last she knew that there was a name for what her mother was.

When he was too ill to take care of himself, Joel checked into the Veterans Hospital, where he obtained free treatment. When he felt better, he returned to his tumbleweed life. Often, he stayed with the Sabloskis, sometimes overnight, sometimes for a week, then months. When he could no longer negotiate their stairs he returned to his mother's house. Belynda saw the toll that that move took on Joel's already depressive state. He deteriorated rapidly and soon was admitted to Southampton Hospital.

By late May 1978, Joel was given morphine on demand for his excruciating pain. For hours on end in the hospital Belynda rubbed his back with a soft bristle brush he favored. They talked about their childhood: the beatings, the terror they had felt, the maggots, the hair rollers incident. And they talked about Belynda's lingering fear of Arlene. "She can't hurt you anymore," Joel told his sister. He encouraged her to stand up to her, yet it had taken him almost twenty-seven years and a terminal illness to do just that.

On one of her visits, Belynda spoke with Dr. Marion outside Joel's room. The cancer had already spread to his lungs, kidneys, liver. He had gone from a strapping one hundred sixty pounds to eighty-seven. The prognosis for what should have been a curable illness looked very bad.

Marion mentioned to Belynda a last-ditch attempt that would involve invasive procedures causing Joel yet more discomfort. "But Joel doesn't want that," Dr. Marion told her. "Joel knows he's not going to go home."

Belynda was furious. "You mean you're just going to let him die?"

"It's inevitable, Belynda. He's let himself get to a point where it is irreversible."

The neglect Joel experienced in childhood had become too ingrained a pattern in his adult life.

On the evening of June 11, Belynda told her brother that she would be late visiting him the following day. After a long absence she had to return to work; but she would be back that evening. At four-thirty on the afternoon of June 12, 1978, Joel succumbed to Hodgkin's disease. Belynda had just returned home from work when her husband Fred took her in his arms and told her. "Joel," she cried, "why didn't you wait?"

That afternoon fifteen-year-old Rosalind was in her bedroom when she saw Joel suddenly "appear." He stood in the doorway, his hazel eyes bright, his golden hair thick and wavy. He didn't say anything. Then he vanished. She knew then that her brother was dead.

For a year after Joel's death, Rosalind continued to "hear" the sound of the cane he used in the middle stages of his cancer, tapping on the wood floors at 40 Adams Lane.

Chapter Sixteen

Christine Boxer* had been living across the street from the Sabloskis on Willis Avenue for a year before she learned that Wade Kirby was Belynda's brother. Both women were young mothers, and their husbands sometimes played golf together. Yet Belynda had not mentioned that Wade was her brother. Christine had met Wade while she was still in junior high school. He had returned home from, she heard, somewhere down South; there were rumors he had killed somebody. Christine, who was a few years younger than Wade, could not believe that the town's pretty boy was a murderer. He was a real charmer, tall and lean and very sexy.

Every female from age twelve on up had a crush on him.

She and her best friend, who worshiped Wade from afar, used to see him in Southampton park selling five-dollar bags of marijuana. Christine had heard that Wade's mother found out what he was doing, got into his stash, and threw out the grass. Then Arlene filled the sacks with catnip and dill. When you smoked it you got a queasy feeling in your stomach and it stank like hell. Christine heard that five guys beat Wade up for selling them the catnip.

Wade sometimes called himself Tex. It was a game, his showing himself as different people. One minute he would talk like a New Yorker, the next like a down-home Southern boy. One day he was here, the next he was gone. To Christine, "Wade was like a silhouette."

In the spring of 1981, Wade Kirby was released from prison, where he had served two years for second-degree burglary, a felony offense. By then he had an extensive criminal history. In addition to his arrest on murder charges in Tennessee for the death of Ella Hall and his subsequent conviction on involuntary manslaughter, Wade had been jailed for a wide variety of offenses, including possession of drugs, larcenies, robberies, assaults, and thefts. Just before a 1978 second-degree burglary conviction, he had been convicted of carrying a concealed weapon and auto theft.

By 1981, when a paroled Wade Kirby was looking for a halfway house, he had had a total of seventeen arrests and eleven convictions (six felony and four misdemeanors) since 1968 when he had been adjudicated for his first burglary. A friend referred him to Anita Mohr.

A widow in her late forties, Anita boarded parolees in her home in the Long Island suburb of Farmingville. She spoke with Wade by phone and found him "forthright and truthful. He seemed like a nice dude, and his recommendations were favorable." As fate would have it, Anita would also provide shelter for Wade's mother twelve years later.

Anita has long considered herself an "underdog person." She has never been one to impose judgment and never has much trouble seeing both sides of any situation. And she considers herself a good Christian. Her affinity for those who have suffered or lived at the periphery of the mainstream stems from her own troubled childhood. Anita's background was Irish and American Indian. Her mother was an alcoholic, a "raving lunatic" who physically abused her, and her father deserted the family. As a child, Anita had been sexually abused by a family friend.

At the time Wade Kirby joined the Mohr household, there were three other boarders: a young woman paroled for manslaughter; a recovering heroin addict paroled for grand theft auto; and another young man whose plea bargain had reduced his sentence to second-degree manslaughter. "I'm very popular for some reason with large, aggressive people," Anita explained. "Something in my personality, I shouldn't wonder."

Wade impressed Anita as a basically good-hearted person. She was won over by his fondness for children and animals, who took to him in return. "It don't matter what the world says about you, if my dog loves you and my kids love you, there's something great in there somewhere."

She saw in Wade a gentleness, a certain compassion for people whom he was close to.

And he was a spectacular cook. His specialty was Cajun foods: Buff Creole, heavy on the cayenne; shepherd pies laced with cinnamon and nutmeg; grape leaves and rice dishes. After he left the Mohr household in the fall of 1982, Anita recalls, "everything tasted like cardboard."

Wade mentioned to her, almost in passing, that he had been found guilty of a murder he had not committed in Tennessee back in 1970. He told her he had passed out in a room and awoke to find a woman dead. "He said his father did it, and that his mother advised him to take a plea. Wade, being an outsider, a so-called 'hippie,' his mother thought he didn't stand a chance of getting off." He pled guilty to involuntary manslaughter in November 1971 and served less than two years.

It soon became evident to Anita that her handsome boarder had two Achilles' heels: women and liquor. "He had an insatiable need for attention and affection from women. But he was a very sexy man, and he had a phenomenal ability to attract women. His girlfriends were all nice women with one thing in common: They were all crazy about him. Wade was a romantic, but he was also a good ol' boy: women are to be treated gently and protected but they shouldn't ask too often where you're going and what you're gonna do."

While in New Orleans, Wade had met an American Indian mystic named Walking Man, who became his mentor of sorts. They took a lot of peyote and LSD. During one hallucinatory episode on the beach, Wade began to dance. He danced for eight hours nonstop in the blazing Louisiana sun, thus earning his nickname Sundance, or Dancer.

At that time he also met Judy Fisk* who he would later claim was his common-law wife. Fisk, or "Nightbird," as she was called, shared Wade's fascination with the mystical. A large, likable girl, Nightbird was, according to Anita, "a voluntary psychic vampire. She got her energy from feeding off other people." As a result she had astounding mental power. Anita recalled Nightbird's splitting a lead crystal ashtray in half using only the power of her mind. Nightbird was also a recovering alcoholic.

Anita related to Wade's "deeply spiritual" side. A self-described "pagan," Wade also practiced "white" witchcraft. He fancied himself a "Wicca" priest, an intermediary between God and practitioners who worshiped the spirit in all living things. The primary tenet of white witchcraft is "And it hurt no one, do what Thou wilt"—meaning one should avoid harm to others.

As kind as Wade was to Anita and her kids, he revealed a different persona when he was drunk. Wade was a mean drunk. He could not control his temper. Sometimes he would channel his aggressive anger into marathon dancing sessions and dance with "every female who could walk. Sometimes he would just break a couple of bar stools." Most times, though, the young man who spoke of mystical quests became quite another person. One bizarre incident stands out in Anita's memory.

Wade had come home late one night with a bleached blonde he had just met in a bar. He announced they were going to get married. The young woman joined Anita and her housemate in the kitchen while Wade passed out in the living room. Suddenly they heard a growling sound. Wade was on his hands and knees, and a large, very heavy sofa cushion was in his mouth. He was swinging the cushion back and forth over his shoulder with his teeth, growling and snarling. Then he flung it. It sailed across the living room and toppled a standing bookcase. "He got on his stomach, sinuously crawling on the floor and I got a cold shiver up my spine. I was suddenly aware I was engaged in something that was not straight-across-the-board Christian."

It seemed to Anita then that the devil was inching his way toward her. Wade grabbed her foot with his teeth and balled up his fist. "I could smell his adrenaline, that's how angry he was."

Anita warned him, "You better not hurt me because if you do there's no way back." She didn't know quite what she was saying, but it stopped him dead.

Wade stood up and ripped one of the legs off the solid oak table, then he passed out. Anita dragged him into the living room. His terrified date ran out the door.

"Somehow," Anita recalls with a smile, "I knew the wedding was off."

Anita figured that whatever Wade's demons, they were born of old wounds, that his pain was festering in a dark place within his soul.

Wade told her that he despised his father. As a child, he had seen Tommy Kirby beat Arlene. He spoke of being "afraid when Daddy came home," of feeling helpless when he saw his mother beaten by his stepdad Bob Lotz, and of running away. He felt inadequate because he could not protect his mother. Once he got so angry he actually saw red. Wade was enraged at Arlene for putting up with that abuse, but he also saw her as a victim.

To Wade, Bob Caris was a "nerd" who was manipulating Arlene emotionally and mentally. She seemed to tolerate it, and that made Wade angrier.

Wade did not mince words in describing his mother as a "domineering woman, manipulative." But for all his criticism of Arlene, he resented any diversion of her attention. He particularly begrudged Belynda. "My mother," he told Anita, "moved heaven and earth to straighten out my sister. She wasn't there for me half as much."

Anita was curious about Arlene Caris. For all Wade's diatribes, Anita was not about to judge a woman she had never met. They had spoken on the phone when Wade first moved in, and their conversations had since progressed into more personal topics: children and marriage. Anita recognized something in Arlene Caris that attracted her.

They met over coffee, and Anita found Arlene "fun and bright." They laughed a lot, had a good time. Arlene would complain about her husband, nothing specific, just the usual husband-and-wife gripes. But Anita sensed that Caris said things to hurt her. Bob Caris sounded overly critical. But then, so was Arlene. The focus of that displeasure was her oldest child, Belynda. Arlene fixated more on Belynda's illegitimate pregnancy than on Wade's felony offenses. Anita found that odd.

Arlene and her younger son seemed to have reached some sort of understanding. "Obviously one does not want one's children necessarily to turn out like Wade did, but I think she accepted that he has flaws like everyone else, and doesn't invest too much emotionally." Arlene extended that virtually blind adoration to her younger daughter, Rosalind. She believed Rosalind's behavior was just a phase the girl would outgrow. Anita felt otherwise. She knew that Arlene did not have the slightest idea who Rosalind really was.

It was obvious to Anita that Rosalind resented anyone Wade was dating; she seemed more like a jealous woman than his sister. Roz boasted of her devotion to Wade. She said she had braved a swamp road infested with alligators and black snakes to visit him at a prison in Florida where he was on death row. However, Wade's rather extensive "rap sheet" detailing his criminal history makes no reference to any incarceration in Florida or a death row sentence.

Wade stayed at Mohr's house until September 9, 1982. That evening he was at the wrong place at the wrong time, at least according to Anita, Arlene and Rosalind. "Wade was set up by a jealous female," Rosalind later explained. That "jealous female" was the daughter of a local law enforcer.

Anita's housemate witnessed at least part of the crime. A manic-depressive who, according to Anita, had been spurned by Wade, the woman had observed a car in their driveway. Inside were three people: Wade, a young woman, and a local drug dealer. They were getting high, and Wade passed out. In a scenario reminiscent of Wade's defense in the Tennessee murder when he awoke to find a dead woman, he awoke, this time to find a raped woman.

Suffolk County police and court records told a different story of what occurred that night. Wade, who was then calling himself James Kirby, and a buddy were cruising Old Medford Avenue in Medford, not far from Anita Mohr's home. They spotted a woman Wade knew who was bringing in packages from her car. The men invited her for a few drinks at Broadstreet, a local bikers' bar. They stayed there drinking until four a.m., then the three returned to her house. Wade's friend discreetly left the car while Wade put the moves on the woman. She resisted.

Wade forcibly had sexual intercourse with her and beat her as she struggled out of the car. She ran into her house and called the police. Her assailant, she claimed, had been high on speed.

The cops went looking for Wade at his Farmingville address, but he was not there. A computer rap sheet showed that he was still on parole for felony attempted burglary. He had only one week left on parole. The following day Suffolk County detectives went to 40 Adams Lane. There they interviewed a seemingly bewildered Arlene Caris, who said she knew nothing of the incident—or where her son was. Wade seemed to have vanished. The rape allegation was made more egregious since he was in violation of parole; Wade was a fugitive from justice.

Anita was not surprised that her boarder blew his parole. She had the sense that in jail Wade Kirby felt a sense of comfort and safety. They often had spoken about his life in prison.

"Don't feel bad for me," Wade told her. "I can handle it."

But wasn't it hard to live, without freedom?

"Not really. I manage. It's comfortable enough. I get what I need."

It was then that Anita realized that Wade was a classic recidivist—he was bound to return to prison. The boy whose childhood had been riddled with chaos and fear and who could not control his impulses must have felt a degree of security in confinement. "Wade likes dangerous people. He's messed up, but a very strong personality. If he weren't so fragmented he would have been a formidable force. But I think that prison supplies him with a unique situation in that it gives him the restraints he doesn't possess and at the same time provides him with steady companionship, with the kind of people that make life exciting."

On May 15, 1983, Wade Kirby was arrested in New Orleans for possession of narcotics and a firearm. When officers there learned of his fugitive status and the charges pending in New York, they contacted the Suffolk County police, and an extradition process was initiated. On June 13, the Suffolk County Fugitive Squad arrived in New Orleans. Wade waived his right to extradition proceedings since, to expedite matters, the city had dismissed the drug charges; rape carried a far weightier penalty.

Wade was returned to New York and installed at the Suffolk County jail. On June 17, he pleaded not guilty to rape. That summer his case went to trial. On September 28, a jury found Wade Kirby guilty of first-degree rape, rape by force. He was sentenced as a persistent felony offender to fifteen years to life.

Wade was transferred from the Riverhead jail to Sing Sing in Ossining, New York, which is the "reception" station for the state's prison system. On March 1, 1984, during Wade's intake interview, the officer described him as "an unkempt persistent felony offender [who related] in unrealistic street terminology offering no insight, remorse or perspective. An admitted alcohol and drug abuser, he claims no enemies within the system. Minimal education. No skills and a lengthy sentence. The image offered is pathetic."

Confinement within the New York state prison system has not had a palliative effect on Wade Kirby. Prison records over the years showed disciplinary problems including fighting, harassment, assault on staff, and threats, even a refusal to take a TB test, which put him in lockdown for weeks. Records also showed that Wade has a common-law wife, Judy Fisk (Nightbird), and three children. Since 1993 he has had no visitors.

Chapter Seventeen

On December 27, 1976, Fred and Belynda's first and only child together, Rebecca, was born. In the Caris household there was also a birth, at least as far as Rosalind recalls. That year her mother, then forty-eight, gave birth to a baby boy. He died two hours later.

"I think I was about thirteen and Mom became ill one night, and apparently she didn't think she was pregnant and she got rushed to the hospital. They got her into the emergency room. The pain she was experiencing was labor pains."

How did Arlene manage to conceal her pregnancy?

"My mother was extremely heavy back then, and she always had a healthy appetite."

Rosalind seems to be the only person aware of Arlene's pregnancy. Arlene herself denies ever having been pregnant by Bob Caris. Yet Rosalind remembers her mother returning from the hospital obsessively possessive of her young daughter. She would not let Rosalind out of her sight. "You know, always holding on to me, going shopping, going crazy with the credit cards and buying clothes. It was scary, because nine times out of ten after she bought me something nice, I would end up getting hit for something."

While part of Rosalind reveled in the attention, "the other half," as she later explained, "was like saying 'Be careful. You might get hit for something.' I mean she could go in and out of depression so easily. One day she'd be up and happy and act as if nothing has happened. And the next day, you would wake up to a total war zone."

Anything could trigger Arlene's anger. Once Rosalind hung underpants to dry over the bathtub. "I got beat from the top of my head to the tips of my toes and had to wear a turtleneck with long sleeves to school because she told me if anybody questioned [me] about it, I would get it ten times worse." When the switches made from tree branches broke, her mother used her fists.

The girl who so vividly recalled her mother's "pregnancy" just as clearly remembers her stepfather fueling Arlene's rages. In Rosalind's version of life at 40 Adams Lane, Bob Caris egged his wife on. "He would encourage her. [He said,]

'I don't think you gave her quite enough, go back and do it again.' He wanted to ship me off to a boarding school overseas but my mother wouldn't let him do it."

By the time she was fifteen, Rosalind had escaped the family tensions by drinking. She became what she called a "power drinker." At the local North Sea Tavern, one of Joel's former hangouts, she could drink just about anyone under the table.

Shortly after Joel's death, Arlene and Bob's arguments over money escalated. Rosalind recalls that her mother began to intercept Bob's mail; often those letters contained investment checks. That year, Rosalind remembered her stepfather's inheriting two hundred fifty thousand dollars. He, however, never learned of that inheritance. "Mom swindled it," Rosalind said. She recalled that when the check arrived, Arlene launched into a buying spree—clothes, furs, jewelry, cars. "My mother was addicted to money. You got your drug addicts and your alcoholics—well, she was a moneyholic. Enough was never enough."

When Caris questioned the cost, Rosalind heard her mother say, "Mind your own business. I'm using my own money."

Rosalind was assigned the task of intercepting the bills, and she tailored her schedule around the postman's deliveries. When her after-school job interfered with that assignment, Arlene had the charge card bills diverted to Belynda's Willis Street address. Belynda did recall receiving her mother's mail and questioning her. Soon after that, Arlene rented a post office box.

Intercepting phone calls demanded a bit more ingenuity. Arlene adapted a system used by the deaf and installed the setup in her kitchen, where she spent much of her time. The telephone ringer was turned off, and a red light flashed to signal that a caller was on the line. If Rosalind was in the kitchen alone, she would tell her mother, "Ma, the light's on, the light's flashing," and Arlene would answer. Invariably the call concerned Caris's finances or her charge bills.

Bob Caris, who spent most of his time in the basement with his ham radio, had no idea of the intricate machinations being engineered upstairs by his wife.

There was nothing accidental about Rosalind's pregnancy in the spring of 1979, when she was nearly sixteen. Arlene had warned her, "If one more daughter gets pregnant without the wedding band and the paper to prove it, she is going to get promptly thrown out on her ass."

Rosalind, Arlene's only unmarried daughter,

figured the remark was directed to her. She got pregnant. It was, she thought, her ticket out.

She was sick and tired of having to stay home to divert the bills and phone calls. She had to cook, do laundry, do the dishes, clean the house—and she ended up being the scapegoat for her mother and stepfather.

Rosalind saw her salvation in Rob Troy,* a schoolmate and drinking buddy two years her senior. He was gawky, unattractive, and easily seduced by the beautiful, dark-haired girl with hazel eyes. The prospect of being pregnant and homeless did not suit Roz, so she concealed her condition from her mother while she and Rob made their plans. Meanwhile, she did not alter her lifestyle. She drank, smoked cigarettes and marijuana, and took Quaaludes, a powerful barbiturate. When Arlene remarked about her increased weight, Rosalind said she was simply eating more than usual.

On Rosalind's sixteenth birthday, Arlene presented her with an "inheritance" check in the amount of sixteen thousand dollars. It was, Arlene told her, money left to her by her father, Bob Lotz, who had died more than a decade ago. Rosalind bought a new Mustang. Shortly before Christmas, a drunk driver ran her off the road. The Mustang flipped over twice. Anyone sitting on the passenger side would have been killed, the police said. Rosalind suffered only minor injuries, but the Mustang had been "her baby," and it was totaled. A very angry Rosalind proceeded to beat up the driver of the other car.

Nonetheless, when the ambulance crew learned she was pregnant, they rushed her to Southampton hospital, and Arlene was called.

The emergency room physician greeted Arlene with the good news. "Well, your daughter and the baby are doing fine, Mrs. Caris."

"Daughter and who? You must be mistaken, my daughter is only sixteen years old."

"Is her name Rosalind Lotz?"

"Yes."

"Well, your daughter is between six and six and a half months pregnant."

That night, Rosalind told one of the nurses, "If you let me walk out of here tonight, you will be having to run an autopsy on me and the unborn child, because my mother is going to kill me."

They kept her two additional days, until Rosalind assumed her mother had cooled down. She had not.

Arlene and her daughter drove back to Adams Lane in silence. Rosalind recalled Bob's first comment, "So, you brought the tramp home?"

He began talking about abortion.

"She's six and a half months pregnant," Arlene said. "She can't have an abortion."

As Rosalind later recalled, Bob commented, "Well, she better be putting the little bitch or bastard up for adoption because trash ain't livin' in my house."

They started fighting. Rosalind screamed, "I'm not getting an abortion, and this baby's not going up for adoption. You don't like it, let me outta here. Let me move out." That, after all, had been her plan. Only the timing had been thrown off.

That night, as Rosalind remembers, her mother beat her.

The following day, she and Rob discussed their moving in together immediately. But Rob was not willing to leave his brother, whom Rosalind had once dated but now despised. A month later, and the second time she was hospitalized for toxemia, Rosalind's obstetrician advised inducing labor. She was bleeding profusely, and her health and her baby were endangered. Since she was underage, Rosalind needed her mother's consent. Arlene refused.

"I brought you into this world," she told her daughter, "and I can sure as hell take you out."

One afternoon, Christine Boxer was hanging laundry on the line when Arlene pulled into the driveway. Despite Belynda's admonitions to beware of Arlene, Christine enjoyed the maternal attention; the two became, for a while, friends.

That day she could tell by the expression on the older woman's face that something was very wrong.

"Nothing's wrong, but I'm just sick and tired," Arlene said when they walked into Christine's house. Arlene's voice was strangely high-pitched. "I work my ass off and I go home to that no-good . . ."

Christine assumed Arlene was talking about her husband, whom she continually derided. To listen to Arlene, Bob Caris was a monster. To Belynda he was a saint. Christine did not know whom to believe.

"Bob was fighting with Rosalind because she sits around on her fat ass," Arlene continued in that unnatural voice. "She doesn't do a thing. Bob told her to do something and Rosalind said she'd pull a knife on him. A butcher's knife."

Christine had not yet met Rosalind, but she had formed an unfavorable opinion from what Arlene and Belynda said. The girl was a spoiled brat, cut school, and was generally disrespectful to adults; and she had gotten pregnant. Still, to pull a knife on her stepfather?

"It's true," Arlene insisted. "Rosalind threatened to kill Bob."

Where was Roz now?

"I dropped her off in town. I had to separate them."

Years later, Rosalind told Christine that she had just returned home and was making herself a tomato sandwich when Bob asked whether she wanted a glass of milk. She didn't like his tone of voice. "I called him a few nasty names. Then he called me a 'no-good whore and slut.' And then he went to get up like he was going to hit me." That's when she pulled a knife from the drawer.

Roz told Christine, "If Mom hadn't come in, I would've killed him."

If Bob Caris had any misgivings about his stepdaughter's illegitimate pregnancy, her baby, Danielle, bore none of that ill will. Bob Caris adored her. The two were inseparable. When Danielle saw "Poppy," she'd give him a big old smile. He would pick her up, hug her, kiss her, read her the comics. The two would sit together at the kitchen table, Bob feeding Danielle her baby food; later he would cut up portions of his own meal to share with her. "Eating with Pop-Pop," Danielle called it.

At work, Caris was full of news about his granddaughter. The hopes he had once expressed about Rosalind he now invested in the little girl. Danielle was the light of his life.

One afternoon Marvin Fields happened to see Caris waiting in his car outside the A&P supermarket while Arlene was shopping. Fields approached the car. There was Bob with the baby on his lap, bouncing her.

"So how's the baby?" Fields asked.

"As cute as can be," Bob said, "I'm crazy about her."

Fields saw how gentle Bob was the child, who was no more than six months old at the time. Caris's colleagues were delighted at his new-found happiness.

Chapter Eighteen

In mid-July 1984, shortly after her twenty-first birthday, Rosalind Lotz accompanied her friend Paula to visit Paula's boyfriend, Randy. Randy was in the Riverhead lockup. He had someone he wanted Roz to meet.

"This guy Tony isn't getting any phone calls and he has nobody to write," Paula explained to Rosalind.

"What's he in for?" Rosalind asked.

Paula said it was a drug charge.

Drugs were no big deal, Rosalind thought. She certainly didn't want another wimp like Rob Troy. "But does he know I have a kid?" Rosalind asked Paula. Danielle was two years old, and most guys split when they found out she had a child.

"Yeah, Tony knows. No big deal."

Rosalind donned a pair of torn jeans and a Spandex tank top and headed to Riverhead with

Paula. Her first impression of twenty-four-year-old Tony Campanella was: "This guy is a hunk. He was pumped up, not too nasty, had a nice physique to him and he was nice-looking, part Puerto Rican, part Italian and Navaho Indian."

Campanella told her about the charges against him. He had been set up. Sold four hits of mescaline to an undercover narc. Said he'd had a drug and alcohol problem since he was fourteen, had always gotten into trouble, but nothing big until now.

Rosalind remained unfazed. After all, he wasn't in for rape, or something more serious, in which case she would probably have said, "I'm busy."

Campanella told Roz that his parents were divorced. He said his mother was a sergeant on the police force in West Miami, Florida. His father was living in Savannah, Georgia. He asked about her family.

Roz replied, "Did you ever see *The Wizard of Oz*? That's how I'd describe my mother—the Wicked Witch of the West."

Campanella thought that was pretty funny, and she left it at that. He was gorgeous, accepted her out-of-wedlock pregnancy, and made her feel like a human being instead of trash.

Two weeks later Rosalind brought her daughter to the Riverhead jail. Danielle took to Tony at once. "It was love at first sight," Rosalind said. He affectionately nicknamed Danielle "Little Bit."

Rosalind and Tony began a relationship of sorts. He was transferred to Fishkill, New York, then to Sing Sing and on to Denamora, near Montreal. A maximum security prison like Attica, Denamora was a nine and a half hour drive from Southampton. Tony and Roz held hands in the visiting area and talked. They were allowed one hug and one kiss. Since they were not married, they did not qualify for trailer visits, where, for seventy-two hours, married inmates were allowed conjugal visits on prison grounds. Rosalind and Tony's courtship was one of enforced chastity.

For all its restrictions, the weekend relationship had an element of comfort for Rosalind. Tony wasn't going anywhere, and despite what she had heard about her boyfriend's short fuse, he was always gentle with her. For once Rosalind was assured of relative consistency and safety—albeit in the presence of armed guards—with another human being.

There was also a familiarity about Campanella's situation. With the exception of Bob Caris, violent men and men in trouble were all Rosalind had ever known. Her earliest memories were of her father, Bob Lotz, beating her mother.

Wade was constantly in and out of jail, and she was missing him terribly. Whereas Campanella would be released in another year, Wade would probably never leave prison alive.

Arlene was not pleased about Rosalind's new love. Campanella was, in her opinion, "a real lowlife." Still, she protected her daughter. She told Caris that Roz was dating an Air Force man stationed nearby.

But Arlene made her sentiments known to Roz. One evening Rosalind was preparing to visit her boyfriend. She turned the ignition of her car; it did not start. She lifted the hood and saw that a tangle of wires had been pulled out. Arlene was standing by the driveway, a self-satisfied look on her face.

Rosalind said, "Either you put those wires back where they belong or I'll just take the damn train up."

"Listen to me, you little bitch, you're not going up to see that no-good, low—"

"You're one to talk!" Rosalind screamed. "At least I'm not trying to kill my husband!"

Rosalind could see the muscles in her mother's jaw working. Arlene replaced the wires in the car, and Rosalind tore off.

On February 23, 1985, Rosalind married Anthony Gerard Campanella in the chapel of Denamora Prison. Before the ceremony, Tony's counselor sat her down. He wanted her to read Tony's rap sheet and the history of his mental problems. He explained to her that Tony was a paranoid schizophrenic with suicidal tendencies. As one of the conditions of his parole, set for August 2, 1985, he must remain on his medication, Elavil and Thorazine. Did she still want to go through with the marriage?

"I told him I'd grown up with a bunch of paranoid schizophrenics, the biggest nut case being my mother."

Rosalind wore a white dress she bought at Caldor's, a discount store that sold everything from auto parts to lace curtains. Danielle carried a small bouquet of flowers.

Despite her marriage, Rosalind had not escaped the turmoil at 40 Adams Lane, where she remained, awaiting her husband's parole. There was no telling what her mother was up to next. Shortly after Rosalind's in-prison wedding, Arlene asked her to go the basement, take the clothes out of the washer, and put them into the dryer. Nothing out of the ordinary. As Arlene remembers, Rosalind flicked on the light, but the bulb was out. Strange, Arlene thought then. She had just replaced the light bulb only a few days earlier.

Arlene reached for the bulb and replaced it again. The basement stairs were instantly illuminated. To her horror, she saw a fishing cord strung at the top of the basement stairway! It could have been either one of us took a tumble down that stairway, she told her daughter. Arlene was convinced Bob was trying to kill her.

Bob was downstairs as usual with his ham radio, oblivious to the commotion. Arlene barreled down the stairs, shouting at him, "If you're not behind the wheel trying to kill me, you're booby-trapping the stairs!"

Rosalind's version differs. She was taking a load of laundry downstairs and suddenly tripped and fell, nearly cracking her skull.

"What the hell is this shit!" she screamed.

Arlene raced from the kitchen to the head of the basement stairs. "What are you talking about?"

Rosalind pointed at the transparent fishing cord—cord taken from her own fishing rod. It was wrapped between the railings of the stairs. "Will you please just get a scissors and cut this thing?" she told her mother.

Arlene began to cry. "Oh, sweetheart. That was meant for me. Bob is trying to kill me."

Rosalind did not believe her. Too much craziness had been going on—the phones, the mail, Mom's cashing Bob's checks and Bob not knowing. "I'm moving outta here," Rosalind said. "I'm not going to get caught in the middle of this crap."

"You're not going anywhere," Arlene snapped. "You open your mouth or you leave and I'll get them to take away Danielle. You're not fit to be a mother."

"You should talk!" Rosalind shouted as she backed out of the driveway. That crazy bitch, Rosalind thought. She resolved to move out the minute Tony got paroled.

On New Year's Day, 1985, Belynda and Fred stopped by the Carises for a short visit. On the ride back home, Belynda's stomach cramps worsened. Since Joel's death four years earlier, she had been in and out of Southampton hospital with various medical problems. At first the doctors thought her complaints were psychosomatic. She was simply mourning the loss of her brother, they told her. But whatever the root of her pain, its manifestations were quite physical. In the past few years she had been treated for cysts on her ovaries, a gastric umbilical hernia, three episodes of blood clots in her lungs, and endometriosis, followed by a hysterectomy.

Now she was anticipating a series of blood tests. Her doctors suspected yet another growth. But Belynda was, at that moment, more concerned about her stepfather.

"Do you think Dad looks all right?" she asked Fred. "He said he lost a lot of weight. He just doesn't look right to me."

"Maybe it has to do with losing his job." Fred had also noticed a change in Bob, but a man was expected to be a little depressed after getting laid off, even if Bob really didn't have to work for a living. ITT had let Bob go in October, not because of his performance, which had always been outstanding, but arbitrarily, because of his age. "It's bound to make Bob feel old the way they treated him."

"Mom told me he's been depressed, but I think it's something else."

Belynda knew that the loss of his job hurt Bob's pride. He had not spoken about it, but Belynda sensed his spirit had been wounded.

"Dad doesn't understand why Sharon stopped writing," Belynda said as they pulled into their driveway. "I just can't figure out that relationship. I would have given anything for a father like that growing up. Anyway, I think he should see a doctor. I just got a feeling it's something physical, too."

Bob had seemed uncharacteristically distant this visit, "spaced out," not all there. With Bob meeker than usual, Arlene seemed an even more formidable presence in the Caris household. She snapped at Bob more than ever, over trivial matters, yet he deferred to her. It was almost as if he was afraid to do otherwise.

Without Bob's warmth, the house on Adams Lane repelled Belynda. Maybe it was time, she thought, to stop banging her head against a brick wall. By now she should admit to herself that her mother would never love her. She was feeling a bit like an abused dog that still returned for its master's love and affection, only to be constantly rebuffed.

In mid-January, Belynda underwent surgery for the removal of two tumors in her uterus; one was the size of a softball, the other the size of a grapefruit. Both turned out to be benign. The day before the surgery, Arlene stormed into Belynda's hospital room.

Through a haze of painkillers Belynda heard her mother say, "You have a hell of a nerve lying there when your family needs you! Get up out of that bed and go home. There's nothing wrong with you. You have no business causing this anguish to your family."

Dr. Jane Marion was making her rounds when she heard the screaming. She hurried down the hallway and found Arlene pacing Belynda's room, ranting about her daughter's "psychosomatic problems."

"Mrs. Caris," Marion said, "I must ask you to

leave this room immediately. Your daughter cannot be disturbed."

"I suppose you know more about my daughter than I do," Arlene shouted. "I can tell you a thing or two about this darling girl of mine."

Belynda was crying hysterically. She had always felt helpless in the face of her mother's rage. And now, already so utterly incapacitated, she had no defense. She was terrified that her mother was going to humiliate her in front of Dr. Marion.

But Arlene did not get the chance. A few moments later, a security guard forcibly removed her.

Dr. Marion took the young woman's hand in hers. "Belynda," she said, "you've got to cut your mother out of your life. You need to stay as far from her as you can."

The physician knew the difficult task Belynda was facing. Like many abused children who as adults maintain proximity to the abusive parent, Belynda still hoped for some sign of affection from her mother. Belynda might be a wife and mother herself, but inside that womanly body she was still a hurt and angry child.

Later that day, the phone beside Belynda's bed rang.

"How's my girl feeling?"

It was Bob. She felt tears well up behind her eyes.

"Okay, Dad. Just a little scared."

He reassured her, but just his voice was enough.

"Are you okay, Dad? Fred and I have been worried about you."

"I'm fine, fine. Now you just get some rest and don't worry about a thing. I'll call you tomorrow."

Belynda heard her niece Danielle in the background. Bob was telling her to "throw your Aunt Beena a kiss."

"Aunt Beena, I'm going to eat with Poppy," Danielle said, after she blew a lip-smacking kiss.

"Oh, aren't you a lucky girl."

"Yes."

The phone clicked.

Those two, Belynda thought, as she closed her eyes. Love comes in unexpected ways.

One evening Arlene was cooking hamburger when Rosalind walked in from her job at the local supermarket. The smell of meat searing under the broiler permeated the kitchen. As Rosalind would later recall, Arlene asked her if she had any money.

"What do you mean, do I have money? Yeah, I have some money, I got paid today."

"Good. I want you to take Danielle out to eat."

"Out where?"

"Just out. I don't want her eating off Bob's plate tonight."

"Why not?"

"Will you do like I say?"

"Not without a fucking good reason. I'm too tired to go out."

"You are not to talk to your mother that way," Bob said, walking into the kitchen. Danielle was dangling from his arm. Rosalind saw her mother hastily conceal a small brown bottle behind a jar of pickles. What the hell was Mom up to now?

Arlene gave her daughter a scathing look.

"C'mon, Danielle," Rosalind said. "We're going to McDonald's. I don't like the menu here." She doused her cigarette in her mother's mug of coffee.

"But, Poppy!" Sitting on her grandfather's lap and eating dinner was a high point of Danielle's day.

"We're having hamburgers here." Bob looked tired and disapproving.

"She's my daughter and I'll do whatever the hell I like with her." Rosalind dragged Danielle toward the door. "Oh, stop whining. We'll get Carvel after."

By the time they returned, Bob was once again occupied in the basement with his ham radio.

Danielle ran downstairs to tell him about her Brown Bonnet cone with sprinkles.

Leaning against the sink, Rosalind observed her mother calmly drinking coffee and reading the paper. "So, Mom. What was that about?"

"I've loaded his food up with old man Romanov's medicine." Arlene did not even look up from her paper.

Rosalind couldn't believe what she heard. "Are you out of your mind!"

"It doesn't concern you. Anyway," Arlene said, "I've been putting drops in his coffee, but I need higher doses and he's complaining about the bitter taste. I have no choice. I've got to put it in his food."

Rosalind had thought she'd seen just about everything when Arlene had cracked Bob on the head with the rolling pin a few months ago. He'd had a terrible concussion. But this was the limit. "Mom, if you hate him so much why don't you just leave him? Why don't you just get a divorce?"

"You don't know what you're talking about. You're too young."

"Bullshit. I'm old enough to know that if I can't deal with somebody to get the hell away from him."

Arlene's face was flushed, a sign of impending explosion. Still, she kept her voice low and controlled. "I am too old to start over again. You think I'm going to throw everything I've ever worked for away?"

"Mom, what judge in the world—first of all, the house is yours. He gave it to you for your first anniversary, in case you've forgotten. I'm living here and I have a baby with me. What judge is going to throw us out?"

"You just keep your mouth shut. And don't let her eat from his plate anymore."

"What am I supposed to tell her? You can't eat Grandpa's food because Grandma's poisoning him?"

"Tell her she's old enough to eat from her own plate." Arlene turned and walked from the kitchen. The discussion was over.

Rosalind remained by the sink, gazing out the window into the backyard vaguely illuminated by a street lamp. For the first time since she had met him, Rosalind felt a kinship, however fleeting, with Bob Caris. They were both prisoners of a crazy woman.

Chapter Nineteen

Belynda's profound sense of rejection and emotional abandonment was reflexive when she thought of her childhood. But now that she was an adult, she could not conceive of any way her mother could really hurt her. Living in such close proximity to Arlene, however, carried with it high risk. It would be through Lori that Arlene would find a brutal inroad into her daughter's life.

The rift that would scar Belynda's relationship with her own daughter began at the Vietnam War Memorial on a cold March day in 1981. When Lori was thirteen, her class took a trip to Washington, D.C. But for Lori, this was more than just a school outing; it was a chance to finally find out who she was.

Ever since she was nine or ten, Lori had been asking her mother questions about her real father, Joe Marena. What had he been like? Did she look like him? Wasn't there a picture of him in his uniform? Any picture at all?

Nothing ever came of her questions, except that Belynda would grow short-tempered and change the subject. On the trip to Washington, Lori was excited and proud. She talked to her two best friends about what little she knew of her father. He had been an Italian American and had died a war hero in Vietnam. He had known he had a daughter, though. Mom had sent him a photo of her right after she was born. He had been very handsome, and they had been very much in love.

Lori had always envied her friends who lived with both their real parents and real sisters and brothers in one house. She had two stepsisters—Monica and Becka, each from different fathers. Even though Fred was the only father she'd known, he was really only her stepdad. But unlike her friends' fathers, her real father was a war hero. At least she had that.

When they arrived at the Vietnam Memorial, Lori and her friends went right to the M list of names. Marena. Joseph Marena. For some reason Lori expected his name to jump out at her, as if he would know she was looking for him and would give her a sign. But Joe Marena was not listed.

There must be some mistake. She looked

through a book of war dead, examined all the names beginning with M. Then she thumbed through the first half of the alphabet, until she couldn't see any more because of her tears. On the long ride back home to Long Island she was silent. All she could think of was—there must be some mistake.

Lori had always prided herself on her scrupulous honesty. Not telling the truth was just about the worst thing you could do. Now she felt like a liar, in front of her friends. The humiliation was devastating.

Lori did not tell her mother that they had gone to the War Memorial or that Marena's name was not among those listed. But from then on she began asking about him in earnest. You must have a photo of him. What about your wedding album? What about the flag they always gave war widows, where was the flag? Where was the wedding ring?

As Lori's questions became more insistent, Belynda grew anxious. She had managed to put the issue of Lori's parentage out of her mind, what with the two other children and her job at the supermarket and volunteering for the ambulance corps as an Emergency Medical Technician every few weeks. She reassured herself that Lori could learn the truth only from her, and that gave her some measure of comfort. Certainly Fred, who had known about Marena when he married Belynda, would never betray her. And Arlene had long kept the secret. After all, it was she who had concocted the story of Joe Marena, "Vietnam Hero," primarily to save face with her Georgia clan.

But whatever excuse Belynda made to herself for lying paled in the face of her greatest fear, that of losing her daughter. She began to wonder who she was really trying to protect—Lori or herself?

For now, she hoped that Lori's teenage obsession with her "real" father would soon pass.

"You just have to trust me," Belynda told her daughter.

"What do you mean 'trust you'?" Lori said.

Fred did not say anything, but Lori knew what he was thinking. Hadn't he loved her like his own? She told him, "Dad, this has nothing to do with you. It has to do with me." The last thing she wanted was to hurt Fred. They'd always joked that she was like his 'son.' They would fix things around the house together, he cheered her on at all her sports events, and if there was something she needed, Lori would go to him. Her mother's moods vacillated, but Fred was solid. He was always there for her.

And, Lori had to admit, while she wanted to

know the truth about her "biological father," as she called Marena, she was afraid of knowing.

The sudden mystery exacerbated long-standing tensions between Belynda and her daughter. Even at a young age, Lori knew her mother was groping. Belynda seemed to have different rules for each child. While Lori was expected to abide by strict curfews and to earn straight A's, it seemed to her that Monica could do whatever she liked. And whenever Monica got into trouble, somehow Lori got blamed. "You're the oldest, you should know better," Mom said. "You should have been watching her. You should have said something."

Belynda was demanding of Lori, and Lori lived up to her mother's highest expectations. She was an honor roll student, bought her own clothes, even paid her way to Holland for a school field hockey match. Still Lori felt that whatever she did was never good enough.

"What does Mom want from me?" Lori often asked her father.

"She just knows you're capable of achieving more than your sisters," Fred would answer. Belynda had often told him that she knew Monica's and Becka's limitations, but that Lori was so much brighter, capable of so much more. Fred sensed that his wife saw in her older daughter a chance to fulfill her thwarted dreams. Dreams dashed by her pregnancy with Lori.

As for Lori, she had no interest in boys—she would remain a virgin until she was nineteen. But on her sixteenth birthday, Belynda insisted she go on birth-control pills. She told Lori, "I don't want you getting pregnant and ruining your life like me."

No way, Mom, Lori had wanted to say. I'm never going to make the same mistakes you did.

Even Kay was concerned about Belynda's over-protectiveness of Lori. Kay knew her cousin needed to feel in control, but control was becoming too much of an issue for Belynda. "Belynda never received love and she didn't know how to give it," Kay later explained. "She thought by telling her kids what to do, feeding them, putting clothes on their backs, that was parenting. She didn't want them to hurt, yet she didn't know how to just put her arms around them and tell them she loved them. If a person doesn't love themselves or if they've never been loved, it's an emotion they don't know how to give."

As Kay saw it, much of Belynda's life had been spent trying to find love in the wrong places. Lori, too, saw the futility of her mother's quest. "Mom was always trying to get people to like her. Even those who treated her badly, like Grandma Arlene." The worst were the Tupperware parties.

Belynda would spend the day preparing the food and arranging it beautifully on the table, and then one or two people would show up. Where were all the people from work that Mom helped out in a crunch?

Still, she'd keep on having those Tupperware parties and keep on doing favors for people who didn't give a damn about her.

A part of Lori felt pity for her mother. Another part was angry at her mother's allowing people to walk all over her. It was the angry part that agreed to accept Arlene's unexpected gift of a thousand dollars; she would use it to buy a much-needed car. As far as Lori was concerned, she had more than earned it.

"Your grandmother is just doing it to piss me off," Belynda told her. "She's just trying to get you on her side."

Belynda worried that Lori was trying too hard to keep up with her classmates who lived in the waterfront mansions, drove sports cars, and wore the most fashionable clothes. She couldn't give those things to Lori, but Arlene could. Money was Arlene's only leverage. And Arlene was all too happy to stoke the flames.

Lori knew that her grandmother thrived on any conflicts in the Sabloski household. She also knew that Arlene gave nothing without expecting much more in return.

A few week later, at the beginning of March, Arlene asked Lori to lunch.

"It's just lunch," Lori told her mother. Arlene had made a reservation at the Salty Dog, a seafood restaurant in the exclusive community of Sag Harbor.

"Be careful," Belynda said.

"I'm not you, Mom. There's no way Grandma can hurt me."

When Lori left to meet her grandmother, Belynda told her husband, "My mother has never, ever asked one of the kids to lunch."

"I know, honey, but I'm sure there's nothing at all to worry about."

Fred would never admit to his wife that he too felt uneasy. Whenever Arlene had the chance to step in, she would make things worse. Whatever she did had an ulterior motive.

Fred thought about taking Belynda to lunch, but that would only give her free rein to worry. Best get her busy around the house. Before she knew it, Lori would be back and all her fears would be allayed.

Fred was in the living room when he heard the car door slam. His first impulse was to join his wife in the kitchen. But he held himself back. There was nothing, after all, to worry about. Best downplay the whole business.

Moments later he heard Belynda shouting,

"How dare you talk to me that way! Not while you're living in my house under my roof!"

Fred raced into the room. Lori's face was red, streaming with tears. Her expression was frightening to look at.

"You want to know what she said?" Lori shouted. "Why should I tell you? How long have you been lying to me—sixteen years?"

Arlene had been smiling as they sat down at a corner table overlooking the harbor. "I want to tell you the truth about your father," she said, even before opening the menu. "Your father is alive. He was never in Vietnam. He lives in Smithtown, an hour away from you. Your mother and father were never married. Your father was married at the time. I was good friends with his wife, Ellie. They were neighbors. Your mother and father were going to get married, but your mother found out he lied to her and was married. Joe threatened to kill your mother and you if she didn't marry him. So your mother had to flee to North Carolina." Arlene's voice was triumphant as she concluded the story. "We came up with this lie to protect you, so you wouldn't grow up feeling illegitimate, so the kids wouldn't make fun of you."

Lori did not say a word. She simply got up and left.

Now she wanted to hear it from her mother.

"Believe what you want to," Belynda said. "If that's what you want to believe about Marena, fine."

"So you're not denying it."

"What's there to deny? You just have to trust me."

"All I've heard is about how you deliberately lied to me about my father, and you can't even tell me the truth now. You want me to trust you?"

"I just wanted to protect you. You were too young. And then when I married Fred, I thought of him as your father."

They were like two high-speed cars gunning for a head-on crash.

Belynda had always been terrified of confrontation. She had always felt helpless in the face of unmitigated anger. And now she felt cornered. There was no place she could run, no place to hide from Lori's rage and raw pain. Suddenly an image flashed into her mind. She was back home with her mother, watching her little brothers beaten for something she, Belynda, had done: putting the crabapple in her mother's coffee. She had had a sickening feeling in her stomach then, just as now, watching Lori hurt from something she, again, had done.

Lori told her that she was going to meet Joe Marena in a few weeks. Grandma had arranged it all for March 28. Then she ran upstairs. She wanted to be alone. Everything she stood for, everything she believed about herself, about her parents, had been shattered within the space of a half hour.

On an impulse, Lori pulled the Suffolk County Telephone directory from her night table drawer. She found her own listing: Marena, L., Willis Avenue, Southampton. She had had her own phone since she was thirteen. Below her name was the listing for Marena, Joe. Kings Street, Smithtown.

How utterly, amazingly stupid of her, not to have even wondered. No, it was not stupidity. It was blind trust. She was tempted to call just so she could hear his voice. But, no, she would wait to meet him face to face.

During the following two weeks prior to their "appointment," Lori spoke to no one in the house but Fred. He was supportive, but she could see he was hurting. Her mother made comments about Joe Marena's being a "son of a bitch," which she ignored. Lori had her own anxieties. Was this man going to accept her? Had he known all along where she lived? Why hadn't he made contact? Did she have to call him "Dad"?

Lori had always been self-conscious about her

weight, and during these weeks she kept to a strict diet. She was working at a clothing store in Riverhead and used her discount to buy a new dress. On the afternoon of March 28, Arlene walked smiling into Satellite Clothing Connections. Lori's stomach churned with anticipation as she followed her grandmother to the parking lot.

Her hand was on the car door when Arlene said she had some bad news. "Your father does not want to see you. He told me he doesn't want any part of you."

What did she mean?

"I called to confirm our appointment and he said he does not want to see you." Arlene looked pleased, as if, Lori thought, she had won.

"You came all the way here to tell me he doesn't want to see me?"

Arlene's voice was soft, her Southern drawl pronounced. "I thought you'd want to come back to my house and talk about it."

"I don't believe you."

"Your father is a jerk," she snapped. "He was very abusive. He knew your mother was just a whore—"

"Shut up! Shut up! I don't want to hear any more. I'm going to get to the bottom of this. I'm going to call him myself."

"You don't have his number."

"It's in the phone book."

"I wouldn't do that," Arlene warned. "Don't push it."

"I'm not my mother," Lori said.

Fifteen minutes later she was dialing Joe Marena's number. A woman answered.

"Hello, is Joe Marena there? This is his daughter, Lori Marena." Her heart was beating so fast she felt certain the woman must hear it.

There was a pause. The woman asked her to wait one minute.

"This is Joe Marena." His voice was edged with suspicion.

"This is Lori Marena. I'm your daughter. My grandmother said you didn't want to see me. I want to know why the hell not."

"Look, Lori. Arlene called me this morning about your being my daughter. I have a houseful of guests. It's a bad time. I didn't even know Belynda had the baby. Last I heard she had an abortion. That's what Arlene told me years ago."

"Well, I am your daughter and I'm alive. And I just found out I have a real father. If you're worried I want something, I don't. I don't want anything from you. I'm just trying to make sense of the pieces of stories I've been told all my life. It's like my whole world has been turned upside down. I just need to know the truth."

There was a pause. "Your mother," Marena

said, his voice softening, "she got cold feet. I wanted to marry her, she backed out. Arlene told her if we came back over state lines she'd have me put in jail for bigamy. I didn't care. I loved your mother. I wanted her to know that. I wanted to prove to her I'd do anything for her. Even go to jail."

Arlene had tried to convince him the baby wasn't his. "I don't know how to say this, but I wasn't the only one your mother was seeing." Then he told Lori what Arlene had said.

"Three strikes and it's a whole new ball game," Kay told Belynda when she married Chuck Waldrop in September 1984. He was husband number four. "He'll have to carry me out in a pine box before I'd go through another divorce." After three abusive marriages, Kay had finally found someone who treated her with love and respect.

Life seemed also to have leveled off for Belynda. They last spoke at Christmas. Belynda's Christmas present to herself every year was a long phone conversation with her best friend and cousin. Any other time she called Kay, it was with bad news.

So when the phone rang and it was Belynda, Kay knew there was trouble.

"Kay, Mom told Lori about Marena. How dare she! Lori's talked to him."

Lori talked to Joe Marena?

"He told her," Belynda's voice broke. "He said he didn't know I was pregnant. Mom told him I was a tramp. She gave him a list of eighteen men, Kay! She told him I had sex with eighteen men. She said any of those men could have been Lori's father. Mom told him right in front of Ellie and his kids. My God, Kay! She told him I had an abortion."

Marena's not knowing about the pregnancy was, in Kay's opinion, a crock of bull. The man had been living next door to Belynda on a suburban street, for God's sake. As for Arlene's evil doings, Kay wouldn't put anything past her. The woman destroyed everything she touched.

"Joe wants to meet Lori. He told her he couldn't today because he had a houseful of guests. But they're going to meet in a few weeks. Kay, what's he going to tell her about me?"

Kay tried to calm Belynda. "Belynda, honey. It was just a matter of time. You couldn't expect to keep this a secret all of Lori's life."

"It was Mom's idea. I was just trying to protect Lori."

Kay knew that Belynda had wanted to tell Lori the truth. She so much wanted to be a good mother. But Belynda was afraid of recriminations. She had always been, probably always would be, afraid of Arlene. But as much as Belynda was afraid of her mother, she was as afraid of becoming like her.

"Belynda, don't tell Lori no different," Kay said. "Lori found this man, now she's listening to his lies. There's something inside of her that needs to believe him, that father she never had. But one of these days she's going to find out what he's like. Let it go, Belynda."

"She's gone over to confront Mom about this. Fred's with her."

"Let her deal with Arlene. You just keep away from that woman." Kay believed right then Belynda would have choked the life out of her mother.

Fred Sabloski was outside raking leaves when Joe Marena pulled up in a shiny new red Corvette. The moment he stepped out of the car Fred knew this was Lori's father. The resemblance was striking. A short, dark-haired, muscular man, Marena amicably shook Fred's hand. Lori smiled, too. Marena looked like Popeye.

"I brought my wife, if that's okay."

Lori told Fred, "See you later, Dad," and kissed him on the cheek.

They had lunch at the swank eatery the Barrister in Southampton. Marena's wife, Donna,* a timid woman, sat quietly as he told Lori about his feelings for Belynda, his marriage to Ellie whom he had since divorced, and his two children, her stepbrother, Joe Jr.* and stepsister Lucy.* Joe was four years older than Lori, Lucy, six years. He and Donna had had a little girl.

Lori felt awkward. Joe Marena wasn't her father. Her father was Fred, had been ever since she was seven years old.

They promised to keep in touch. Marena sent the occasional card, but after a while he did not respond to Lori's letters. Years later Lori would meet her stepbrother Joey and through him forge a familial bond with the Marena family. But it would take far longer for the rift between Belynda and Lori to begin to heal.

Chapter Twenty

On the morning of March 29, Rosalind's alarm went off at six, a half hour earlier than usual. She was expected to be at work by eight o'clock, but first she had to drop Danielle off at Southampton College's preschool program. Getting her daughter ready took time.

First thing every morning, Danielle asked about Poppy. Before she was even out of bed: "Is Poppy up?"

Rosalind would answer, "You won't know till you get dressed."

Danielle would hurriedly dress, then scamper down the stairs, shouting, "Poppy!"

Most times Bob was already up, waiting in the kitchen with the morning comics, which he read to her at breakfast. Sometimes he'd play possum and pretend to still be sleeping so that Danielle would jump up on the bed and wake him up. "C'mon, Pop, Pop! Time to get up!"

Rosalind had to admit that whatever she felt about Bob, he was damn good with the kid.

This morning Rosalind wanted some time to herself before Danielle cranked up the day. She lay in bed, enjoying the quiet while her daughter still slept. Bob and Mom had had a hell of a fight last night. More screaming than usual. Mom with her stories, getting everybody into trouble. Bob must have gotten hold of the phone bill, all those collect calls from Tony from prison. Or it could have been the mail.

"Mrs. Rosalind Campanella. Figures." Rosalind would later recall Bob saying. "Trash marries trash."

Rosalind was glad he had found out. It was hard keeping up with Mom's stories. First it was one thing, then another; how could she keep it all straight? So Rosalind told him. Yeah, they got married, in prison. So what? Tony was getting out in August. He was coming to live here with her.

"Over my dead body," Bob said.

Fine. She and Tony would find another place to live. Then Mom put in, "You're not going anywhere."

If Bob had gotten hold of the mail, he probably knew about all the money his wife was stealing from him. Well, served her right. Mom didn't care what she put anyone else through as long as it was peaches and cream for her.

Rosalind heaved herself out of bed, suppressing a wave of nausea. Tony seemed happy about her being pregnant. Told her he didn't have no kids. She said, Yeah, right. Anyway, abortion was out of the question. To her, that was murder. Anybody who gets an abortion oughta do time in jail.

Rosalind decided to get some ginger ale to calm her stomach. She was heading down the stairs when she saw her mother by the front door, crying.

"Mom, what is it?"

Rosalind would later remember seeing bruises on her mother's face and arms.

"Did he do that to you? That son of a bitch! I'm going to tell him—"

Arlene grabbed her arm. "Don't go in the bedroom. You don't need to."

"Oh, yes, I do."

"No, don't." Arlene gathered herself and wiped the tears from her eyes. "The problem is solved," she said.

What did that mean?

"Don't worry about it. Just get little Danielle dressed, fed, get her to school. Call in work and see if you can get the day off. Tell them it's a family problem."

"What I am supposed to tell Danielle? She's gonna be asking for Poppy, Poppy."

"Tell her Poppy's not feeling well."

Great, Rosalind thought. Now she has me lying to my kid. There had better be a good reason.

Rosalind dropped Danielle at the curb by the preschool. She hated going in there, with all those Southampton snoots. She was more of a beer-and-pretzels girl. When she returned to the house, Arlene called her into the master bedroom.

Rosalind walked in. "Holy shit! What happened?"

There was blood on the blankets, on the wall. Rosalind looked from the bulky form bundled up on the bed to her mother. Arlene was wiping the gun with a corner of the sheet. "Oh, my God. You shot him. You killed him!"

"It was in self-defense." Arlene was very calm.

Rosalind thought she was going to throw up. "We gotta call the police," she said.

"There's no way in hell we're calling the police. I'll lose everything."

"Mom, what are you going to do with the body? We gotta call the police."

Arlene lifted the Mossberg and pointed the barrel between Rosalind's eyes. It pressed cold against her forehead. "You open your mouth and you're next," she said. She told Rosalind to pick up Danielle at lunchtime, then drop her off at one of her girlfriends' houses. See if Danielle could spend the night. "I need time to think about we're going to do."

Rosalind wanted to know, what did she mean "we"?

A few days later, Arlene stopped by Ellie Marena's house in Lake Ronkonkoma. Ellie and Joe had long since divorced and Ellie had remarried, but she and Arlene remained friends. Arlene told Ellie that she had several guns she wanted to get rid of. No use cluttering up the house, and Danielle was getting into places she shouldn't. Would her husband be interested? One of them was a Mossberg .22. No charge, a gift. She knew he collected guns. Ellie said no, he wasn't interested.

On April 8, Tony phoned Rosalind collect from Denamora Prison. He had received the letter she wrote only the day before. Great mail service, but was this some kind of joke?

It was no joke, Rosalind said. Mom had put Bob up in the attic cubbyhole. Just until they figured out what to do with him. A quote unquote temporary situation.

"You're serious?"

Yeah, she told him. But don't worry. Nobody'd think you had anything to do with it.

Tony said, "You better find a way of getting rid of that before I come home." He lowered his voice. "Because no way I'm gonna live in a house with a dead body in it."

Rosalind said she couldn't blame him. It was starting to get to her, too. And it had been heavy as hell dragging that thing upstairs.

Tony's phone time was up. She said she'd write him. Love you, babe. On April 9, Tony received another letter from his wife.

Dearest Sweetheart, (I love you with all my K)

I got your tape today. So, it will be here when you come home in a few months. I am so mixed up inside. I don't know what to do about this SHIT! What happened *here!!* I can't sleep much at night anymore. I hate being in this house period!!

I've been wanting to talk to you but, was afraid to. I also knew I couldn't keep it from you *either!?!? So Sweetheart, what do I do about this Shit!* I know, I'm not the one who got rid of the problem *but*, I know about it and I didn't or better yet couldn't report it! You know why I couldn't tell anybody, but my Loving, sweet, darling, husband (that means you) I need to hold you, and kiss you.

I know you don't like hearing this all the time,

but I need to be with you. I can't stand being so far away from you. I know it's driving you *FUCKIN' NUTS* also. Hopefully Mom will give me the money to go and see you in May.

I know it sounds like a long time but it will pass, quick I hope (don't you!). Well, Danielle sends a big hug and kiss to her daddy. Mom says hi and to *stay out* of the BOX!?!?! I love, need, and want you very, very, very much, please never forget, *Please!*

See you soon, I hope!

Love Always For Ever & Life for Eternity

Rosalind & Danielle

P.S. Please help me! tell me what I do.

The Porter family reunion was held on Memorial Day weekend in Dayton, Tennessee. A tradition for generations, the reunions had petered out about forty years earlier. Through Kay Waldrop's efforts, the clan once again got together, this time in the town where, sixty years ago, Darwin's theory of evolution had been challenged in the notorious Scopes Monkey Trial.

Family from Spring City and Dayton, Rossville, Atlanta, and Ringold, Georgia, gathered at the Porter cemetery, the site where in the early 1880s, Arlene's great-great-grandparents' staked their claim to Tennessee farmland. Then they caravanned to Belle and Blaine Porter's* home, a Georgian plantation-style brick structure surrounded by rolling green hills outside Dayton. Blaine, a cousin of Arlene's father, Clard Porter, had done well for himself.

Kay was helping Belle dish out the fixings: fried okra, green tomatoes, pickled spiced apples, fried chicken, meat loaf, thick slices of ham—when Arlene pulled up in a brand-new maroon and gray van. Kay watched her aunt stride toward the picnic tables, all smiles, "like she was Queen Mary and everybody was her court." After perfunctory hellos, Arlene told the family that she had "only paid $25,000 cash" for the van. In that "Park Avenue" accent, Kay said to herself.

It was Arlene's first attendance at a family reunion, and she was bearing armloads of gifts. Clara, whose birthday was May 30, received four collector plates, which Kay figured were worth a pretty penny. Those who knew Arlene only as "one of Clard's daughters who lived up North" listened with fascination as she talked about Southampton, her beautiful home, and her husband's trip to Saudi Arabia, where he had since fallen ill. A heart attack, she told Belle Porter.

Wasn't she concerned about her husband? Belle asked. Why wasn't she at his side?

Arlene said, "I am in constant contact with the doctors, who are the very best specialists in the world. We are in communication by ham radio, one of my husband's hobbies. I am confident he is getting the very best care."

And what about her handsome son?

"Oh, Wade is doing well for himself. He's a chef in Louisiana for a very expensive restaurant."

Arlene's voice dropped when one of her cousins asked about Joel.

Joel died, she told them, in June 1978. "It was his wish that his ashes be scattered at sea, which he loved. And so my daughter, Rosalind, and I took a boat across the Long Island Sound especially for that purpose."

Johnny Luke's grandkids, Tommy* and Cindy*, were sitting across from Arlene and Kay. Six-year-old Tommy took a bite of his spiced apple; he made a face and set it down. His three year old sister, a blond cherub of a girl, took a slice of the apple from her brother's plate.

Suddenly Arlene reached out and grabbed the apple from Cindy's mouth. "Don't you ever do that again! Never ever take food from somebody else's plate, young lady."

The table fell silent. Cindy began to cry. The child was clearly terrified. "Arlene had gone ballistic on that little girl," Kay later recalled. "I could have choked that woman myself."

Later in the day, Arlene and Clara were in the kitchen making coffee. Arlene was telling her sister about some recent large purchases, among them the van.

Wasn't she spending a lot? Clara asked. What with Bob being sick, weren't there bills to pay?

"I've got plenty of money," Arlene said. "I've been cashing some of Bob's stocks and bonds."

Did Bob know what she was doing?

"What he doesn't know won't hurt him," Arlene replied.

That wasn't right, Clara said to herself. Myrtle had had nothing till she married Bob Caris.

Released on parole on August 2, Tony Campanella strode into 40 Adams Lane wearing biker boots, torn jeans, and a leather jacket. His hair was shoulder-length, and a bandanna was wrapped around his forehead. He looked to Rosalind like something out of an old biker movie. A real Hell's Angel.

From the moment they met, Tony and Arlene had despised each other. Given the animosity, Rosalind thought it best not to tell her mother that Tony knew about the body. She had a feeling that the less Mom thought Tony knew, the better.

She herself was petrified of her mother, not just because of what she had done to Bob, but also what she had done to Brandy. Rosalind had gone up to visit her husband on her birthday,

July 11. When she returned, she found her golden Lab in the garbage can, his head blown off.

"I shot the damn thing because he was tearing up my garden," Arlene told her.

"To me," Rosalind would later say, "*that* was the breach of trust."

Meanwhile, Bob's body remained in the attic. The problem of disposal had been discussed intermittently throughout the summer, but no satisfactory decision had been reached. Arlene talked about an acid she could buy through her private-duty nursing connections; it would melt down flesh, right to the bone. Rosalind could then ditch the bones along one of the back roads she took to visit Tony up at Denamora.

Rosalind said, "Hell, no."

There was some talk about putting the body in the foundation of a pool a neighbor was building. They could dump it late at night, and when the cement was poured nobody would be the wiser.

"Ma, you hate swimming pools," Rosalind said.

Somehow that reason sufficed and the plan was abandoned. The body remained in the attic cubbyhole at the rear of Rosalind's clothes closet.

After a while it became clear to Rosalind that

her mother believed her own stories about Bob. Roz could hear it in the way Mom talked to Belynda on the phone. So smooth, so easy for her. "Bob decided to take a vacation to Saudi. . . . Yes, by himself. . . . He had a heart attack. . . . No, he's better. He's gone to San Francisco to see Sharon. I flew out to see him but I got a cool reception from Sharon and I have no interest in staying where I'm not welcomed. . . . No, he flew straight back to Saudi. I put him on the plane at Kennedy. His heart condition took a turn for the worse so he is consulting specialists there."

Arlene bought two hundred dollars' worth of Airwicks. It looked like the body was not going anywhere.

The hell with it, Rosalind said to herself. It's her problem, not mine. There was no point in thinking about it. She had her own life to deal with. She knew Tony was off his medication, and whoring around with anything he could get his hands on, mostly teenage girls. What did he think, it wouldn't get back to her? This town was nothing but an oversized Peyton Place. People here didn't like ex-cons messing with their daughters.

Now Mom was saying Tony was coming on to her. Tony said Mom was coming on to him. Rosalind decided to get herself a career and move out, just her and Danielle. She planned to take the test to enter the police academy in the fall. She'd become a cop. To hell with both of them.

Mom seemed pleased. She said she had been a member of the force in New York City, years before Roz was born.

"You better get rid of that lowlife first," Arlene told Rosalind. She suggested an annulment. Roz said she would think about it, but she still loved the man.

During the summer, Christine Boxer had noticed Arlene's new van pulling into Belynda's driveway, two, three, often four times a day. They must be on better terms, Christine figured. Belynda had been all torn up over the incident with Lori and consequently had stopped speaking to her mother. It certainly wasn't Arlene's place to tell Lori about her real father, and Christine could understand Belynda's anger and hurt. Still, she had a hard time figuring those two out. Belynda spoke as if she hated her mother, but she continued to let Arlene into her life.

Maybe Bob's illness was bringing them together. Arlene seemed confident that her husband was on the mend, but Belynda was worried.

"I don't know," Belynda told Christine. "Something is just not right."

In midsummer, hurricane Gloria wrecked havoc along the coast of Long Island. Power lines were torn down, houses along the rocky shores were swept under tides, and huge trees were uprooted as if by some giant hand. The Caris home suffered minor damage, but Arlene decided to reshingle. Belynda stopped by to see how the work was going.

She had not been to Adams Lane in months, not since that blowup with Lori. She told herself that was it, she would never speak to her mother again. But somehow Arlene managed to insinuate herself back into her life, always finding some reason to stop by the Sabloskis. As Belynda entered her mother's house through the kitchen door, she thought she would vomit. What the hell was that smell?

"A dead animal in the walls," Arlene said. "They must have reshingled over it."

"Get an exterminator, would you?" Belynda noticed bottles of Airwicks set on every step leading to the second floor. Dozens of Stick Ups were on the walls. "How long have you had these, Mom?"

"Ever since it started smelling bad."

The pungent odor of artificial pine mingled with the stench of the dead animal and at least a week's worth of garbage piled up in the kitchen.

One thing was sure—Mom had better get the place in order before Bob came back.

On the evening of September 7, Fred returned home from work to find his wife collapsed in tears in the kitchen. She told him Bob was dead. A sudden heart attack.

"I don't understand," Belynda said. "Something is just not right. He suddenly goes on vacation alone? Honey, you know Bob never goes anywhere without Mom. Then he gets sick, he gets better, he flies to see Sharon in California, Mom flies out to see him. He doesn't come home, he goes back to Saudi. Now he's dead?"

Belynda told her husband that she had spent all day with Arlene. Mom had had her hair done, then gone shopping for clothes. "I thought I better stay with her. I thought she was just in shock, that it was going to hit her suddenly and I better be there. Nothing, she had no reaction at all."

Later that night, Belynda went to see her friend Geri McLaughlin, who worked at the pharmacy at Southampton hospital. Maybe Geri could figure this whole thing out; she was very down to earth. Something was strange, Geri agreed.

"I know you're going to think I'm crazy," Belynda said, "but I think Mom killed Dad."

"I don't believe that," Geri said.

* * *

Early the following morning Rosalind heard Tony and Arlene downstairs arguing. Tony must have just come in. He hadn't been home last night. Or the night before. With him off his medication, there was no telling what he was doing. Rosalind had a pretty good idea, though. Day and night there'd be someone banging at her door, looking for Tony. Tony owed drug money. Tony was screwing this guy's girlfriend, that guy's daughter, some other guy's wife.

"Where's your brother?" they wanted to know.

"He ain't my brother," she told them, "he's my husband"—which made some of them real hot under the collar.

The father of one seventeen-year-old girl told her, "You better start looking for a cemetery plot for your husband."

Fine with her.

Rosalind heard the arguing downstairs getting worse. What now? She heaved herself out of bed.

Tony's eyes were red and bloodshot; he had probably been up doing drugs, drinking, screwing Michelle or Candy or whoever.

Tony was glaring at Arlene. "If I don't get what I want, I'm sure the cops would be very interested in your little secret upstairs."

Rosalind felt a cold wave of nausea. She could see that her mother was in shock.

"I didn't tell him, Mom," she quickly said.

"You think I can't find a goddamn dead body in this house?" Tony said. "Dead mice in the roof, right?"

"You got a hell of a nerve," Rosalind shouted. "You're off screwing around, flaunting it in this town where everybody knows me. Mr. Big Shot around these little shits. And now you're fuckin' blackmailing my mother!"

Tony looked at his wife as if he had just noticed she was in the room. Rosalind burst into tears. "Why did you even marry me?" she said.

"It was a good idea at the time," Tony said.

"Meaning what?" But she knew what he meant. A wife and stepdaughter would look good to his parole officer. A rich bitch from Southampton, with a mother who was Mrs. Moneybags.

"So you better come up with some heavy cash," Tony told Arlene.

"You bastard!" Rosalind screamed. "You don't care anything about me. You come home drunk, change your clothes, and you're gone." To think she had loved him. Was still in love with him. "Well I can tell your parole officer a thing or two."

Rosalind saw his eyes get strange. Mom must have seen it too, because she picked up the phone, told Fred and Belynda to come right over, Tony was going to do something crazy.

Tony suddenly turned and strode out the door. Arlene followed. She's going to give him what he wants, Rosalind said to herself. Mom was going to give that scumbag money that should, by rights, be hers. Money that Mom was spending on more clothes, furs, jewelry for herself.

She had had it. She was tired of being everybody's dupe. They were nothing but users, both of them, Tony and Mom. Good old Roz, everybody's punching bag, everybody's scapegoat. Good old Roz, keeping all their dirty little secrets. What was she getting in return? Nothing, except maybe a murder rap. Turned in by her own whoring husband. She'd be damned if she was going to prison for something Mom had done.

Several minutes later, Belynda and Fred walked in and Rosalind knew then what she was going to do. She was going to let Belynda in on Mom's little secret. Mrs. Sabloski would be more than happy to turn in Mrs. Caris, a.k.a. Mom.

Chapter Twenty-one

September 16, 1985

Brockett's Funeral Home, on tree-lined Hampton Road in Southampton, was a large Victorian gingerbread house with majestic gables and a wide veranda on which potted palms were placed in summer. Its grounds were manicured, pristine.

A week after the murder and the completion of the autopsy, Robert Caris's body was sent to Brockett's, where it was arranged in a coffin that Belynda and Fred had selected. In the early evening of September 16, while smoky amber light filtered through the beveled windows, friends and family filed into the paneled foyer to pay their respects.

Early that morning Belynda had picked up Sharon Wheeler at the airport. Over the years Belynda had heard about Bob's adopted daughter, but the two had never spoken; that morning they met for the first time. Driving to Kennedy Airport, Belynda was apprehensive. Bob had often spoken about Sharon's refinement, her intelligence, the luxury in which she had been raised. Belynda felt intimidated by that kind of sophistication. The "correct" placement of a knife and fork was the extent of her own table etiquette. Sharon had gone to a finishing school in Switzerland, while she had been raised by a hillbilly from Georgia.

In turn, Sharon knew virtually nothing about the Kirby family. Years later she would contend that her father learned of Belynda's existence only after the marriage, that he had no idea of the extent of Arlene's family or their personal histories. On the evening flight from San Francisco to New York and her father's funeral, Sharon recalled a letter he had sent about ten years into his marriage with Arlene. He wrote: "I know now that I have made the biggest mistake of my life."

The meeting between the women was strained. Sharon was exhausted and still shaken from a car accident she had had on the way to catch her flight. As Belynda exited onto the Long Island Expressway, Sharon said in an accusatory tone, "Your mother killed my father."

Several hours later, while Sharon was resting at the Sabloski home, Belynda mounted the steps of Brockett's Funeral Home. She pushed open the heavy oak doors and stepped into a polished foyer that smelled of lemon oil and sweet flowers. Since the morning of September 8, life had lost all its familiarity. Her presence at the elegant funeral home had a dreamlike quality that muted her every waking hour.

The last time she had been in Brockett's was for Joel's wake seven years ago. Arlene had said that Joel did not want to be buried, that he wanted his ashes cast across Long Island Sound; she had promised to carry out his wish. For Joel's' wake, Arlene had requested an open casket. When Belynda saw her golden-haired brother, his face at last free of pain, she wept bitterly, for his short life and their so hurried reunion. But Arlene did not shed a tear. Not one. She stood beside Joel's coffin taking pictures of him. So calm, like she was at a picnic.

No wonder Joel wanted to be cremated and tossed to the wind, Belynda thought as she watched their mother taking flash photos. Cremation was the only way he would be free of Mom.

This morning, Fred and several of their friends were waiting for Belynda. The moment she saw her husband she knew something was wrong.

Fred gently took her arm. Paul Brockett, the

owner of the funeral home, looked uncomfortable.

"Belynda, honey, Mr. Brockett needs to ask you something. I think you'd better sit down."

She sat on a hard bench in the foyer.

"Belynda," Paul Brockett said, "would you like Joel buried with Bob?"

"I beg your pardon?"

"Do you want your brother, Joel, buried with Mr. Caris?"

What was Brockett talking about? Joel had been dead for seven years. His ashes had been scattered at sea. Her mother and Rosalind had taken the Port Jefferson ferry across to Connecticut for just that purpose.

"No, Belynda. Your brother has been abandoned here for seven years. His remains are still here. They were never claimed. We don't have to talk about this now, but maybe after."

Abandoned? She found her voice. "No, I do not want Joel buried with Bob, and I want to talk about this right now."

Brockett told her there was no money involved in claiming Joel. "All you have to do is sign a piece of paper and you can take the remains. You can take him home."

All these years, Belynda thought as she walked into Paul Brockett's office. All those lies.

* * *

On the night of Bob Caris's funeral, Willie May decided there was no sense in trying to sleep. For the first time in four decades she felt the physical distance from her sisters and brothers who had never left the South. They had always been able to console each other during the various upheavals that occur in large families, even at long distance. But for what Myrtle Arlene had done, there was no consolation; there was no emotional defense. There were only the aching questions that had been plaguing Willie May ever since Belynda called ten days earlier. Should they all have taken Myrtle's tales more seriously? Were there signs all along that she was capable of murder? Could they have stopped her?

Now their family was destroyed.

Willie May wished she could hate her sister. It would be so much easier if she could.

Her hands felt heavy as she began a letter to Clara that she had been formulating in her mind for days.

Dear Clara:

I'll apologize first for writing such a depressing letter. These things are so heavy on my heart and mind that somehow I have to have some answers. I just wonder if you and Alice have the same feelings and how you are handling them. I tell myself Arlene deserves any punishment she gets for the horrible crime she committed and she doesn't deserve any compassion from us but I still feel it for her. Every time I think of her being in jail and how depressed and alone she must feel my heart aches for her. While I hate the crime she committed I guess I still love her. She is still our sister. My big problem and question is how far we as her sisters and brothers should go?

You have probably seen the newspaper clippings I sent down to Heartsell. Maybe they helped you justify some of your feelings. There are some more things that have come up since those were printed. I think I told you about the pills she had and tried to get Belynda to destroy. The police has those. She also wrote to Bob's daughter about Bob and how much she hated him. She also alienated his two brothers against him. It just seems as though she was planning on doing something to dispose of him for quite some time. I don't think she actually planned on shooting him but things just climaxed that way. I don't think there is anything I can do to help her out of this mess but I won't do anything to hurt her either. I still hurt, I get angry and sometimes it is all I can do to keep from crying. I think of Belynda and her family, of the hurt that they have gone through. Right now Belynda is at the hate stage. I know she will get over that and that is when everything is going to hit her very hard.

I feel guilty because I don't seem to have much feeling for Rosalind at all. I still feel she was the cause of all the hostility between the two. I never really knew her so maybe that is why. I don't know. I only know I need some answers and don't now know where to get them. I really think it will help all of us though if we can discuss our feelings among us and maybe then we can find the answers.

Clara, please answer and let me know how everyone down there feels. I need to talk to someone and I'm sure you do too.

Love and May God Bless.
Willie

Despite Arlene's enforced departure from the Caris house, Rosalind remained at 40 Adams Lane. With two young children, no job, and an absent husband, where was she supposed to go? But she found any excuse to avoid staying at the house. She spent hours driving around, sometimes looking for Tony, often protracting errands into half-day excursions. Most times she just drove, not knowing where she was going. One thing she knew, she did not want to be in that house alone. It spooked her.

During one of Rosalind's absences Belynda returned to the Caris home. Investigator Don Delaney had asked her to look around in hopes of finding further incriminating evidence. What Belynda saw stunned her.

It wasn't so much the filth in which Roz was living—the stench of dirty laundry, the rotting food, the piles of garbage in nearly every corner. It was a more profound sense of decay. The house at 40 Adams Lane had finally revealed itself. The rage and sadness and distrust that had festered within its walls were now manifest. The house had given up its secrets. It was showing the world the psychic horrors that it had long concealed.

The stench of decomposing flesh seemed embedded in its very structure. Some of the walls were punctured with fist-size holes, marks of Tony's temper. In a way, this devastation was a form of closure, Belynda thought. Her mother had killed the man who loved this house, and now Rosalind was finishing the job. Rosalind was stripping away the last vestige of Bob Caris's dignity.

As Belynda walked from room to room, she could not shake the feeling that someone was watching her. There was a cold sensation at the back of her neck unlike anything she had ever felt. It was eerie but not frightening. Apparitions and ghosts did not frighten her. A year after Joel died, Belynda had brought her girls to stay over at their grandparents' while she and Fred went out for the evening. She had tucked in Lori, Monica, Becka, and Danielle, who wanted to sleep with her cousins, and then walked downstairs to the living room. Joel was sitting on the couch. Her first thought was, "Oh, what's Joel doing here tonight?"

He looked at her and smiled with the same eyes as hers. "You're going to be all right," he said. Then he vanished. As sudden as the flip of a light switch, he was gone.

"I'm not all right, Joel," Belynda now found herself saying aloud. "I'm fatherless and motherless. It feels like it's the end of my life."

That odd sensation of being watched followed her into the master bedroom. The room appeared to have been divided by some invisible line. On Arlene's side, dirty clothes were heaped in random piles stretching from the doorway to the back wall. Dirty clothes were piled on her side of the bed higher than the bedpost.

But Bob's side of the room was immaculate. He might have walked through the door at any moment, slid open a drawer of his highboy and selected a starched white shirt and a neatly folded undershirt, opened his closet and slipped a pair of perfectly pressed khakis off a hanger, chosen a pair of polished shoes from a regimental row.

Was this some kind of shrine? Belynda wondered. Or was this demarcation a line that not even her mother could cross? The sink in the master bedroom overflowed with prescription bottles: sleeping pills, diet pills, tranquilizers, antibiotics. Some of them were in Arlene's name; others were in names Belynda had never heard of.

Throughout the first floor, strewn across the stained carpet and wood floors, were paper bags and suitcases. Belynda opened one after the other. There were bank statements, IRS forms, stock receipts, several Social Security cards in her mother's various surnames: Myrtle Lotz, Arlene Lotz, Arlene Caris. Two cards had totally different ID numbers. There were receipts from Bridgehampton National Bank, European American Bank, Marine Midland, Chemical, and Bank of the Hamptons; many multiple accounts in her mother's various surnames. Belynda also came upon receipts from Aramco. Mom had been cashing Bob's retirement checks while he was dead in the attic.

Belynda could not bring herself to go upstairs. She would call Delaney and he could get his search warrant. She had seen enough.

That evening Belynda and Sharon were folding freshly laundered clothes, piles of children's clothes in primary colors that were reassuringly cheerful. The daily task anchored the women in a familiar, shared reality. A few hours earlier, Sharon also had returned to Adams Lane. It had been twenty-one years since she had last been to her father's house. The occasion had been her mother's death. She had not visited her father and Arlene in the fourteen years of their marriage. "I had not been invited," she told Belynda. Belynda thought that odd.

Sharon, too, had been shaken by what she saw. The worst part was the letters, her letters to her father. They were stacked a foot high on the silver buffer, piled on end tables, on the couch, under the couch. Dozens of letters. Each and every one, some postmarked as early as October when James left, were still unopened. There was a Father's Day card she sent in June, almost three months after the murder; it had been opened. Sharon recalled that Arlene had written back, "I hope your father will thank you for this one!"

Arlene, Sharon learned, had put her own name on the deed to the Southampton house—shortly before the murder.

By the end of Sharon's stay, the two women had had enough of each other. Sharon could no longer bear Belynda's continual crying. Belynda could not tolerate the accusations in Sharon's voice.

* * *

Tony Campanella had been erratic in his communications with his wife, but he was keeping in close touch with Investigator Don Delaney. He wanted to make sure that he was not associated with his mother-in-law's crime. The week of the funeral Tony offered Delaney additional information. He told the investigator that in early September, Arlene had spoken to him about her future plans.

"She said she got a job offer in a medical center in Boston," Campanella said. "Two people she worked for before were going to pay her almost a thousand bucks a week to be their private nurse."

So Arlene had gotten herself a job as a nurse? Delaney prompted.

"That's right. In Boston."

Did she give you any names, addresses?

"No. She sounded kinda vague, but she was going to make a lot of money. So, you know, she was happy."

At Arlene's request, Campanella rather reluctantly visited her in jail. She spoke about a bank account she had opened in Boston.

"It's in a name nobody knows," he told Delaney. "She said it's enough money to last her for a while. For a good while."

* * *

Don Delaney was not surprised when, shortly after the funeral, Belynda Sabloski called with yet more evidence of her mother's culpability. During the past week, Delaney's respect for Belynda had deepened. Here was a very attractive, well-kept suburban woman who cared deeply about her family. Yet in only a few days, her entire life as she had known it had collapsed. "I just want to know the truth," Belynda told Delaney that morning when she came to file yet another statement. He knew that the truth—as devastating and painful as it was for Belynda, was her only hope for emotional repair. The lady had courage. And her quest for the truth had made her an invaluable partner in the murder investigation.

Delaney felt certain he now knew the motive for Caris's murder. He had, he believed, an airtight case for second-degree, premeditated murder.

Chapter Twenty-two

April 10, 1986

More than one year after the murder of Bob
Caris, Belynda Sabloski and Investigator Don
Delaney entered the Suffolk County Courthouse
in Riverhead. Arlene Caris was scheduled to appear this morning before Judge Thomas V. Mallon for sentencing.

A month earlier, District Attorney William
Ferris had accepted a plea bargain from Arlene's
defense attorney, William De Vore. Bill Ferris
agreed to a plea of first-degree manslaughter.
Manslaughter in the first degree allowed for mit-
igating circumstances, like extreme anger, under
which a murder was committed, but it would also
ensure Arlene's imprisonment, quite possibly up to
twenty-five years. She was already fifty-eight years
old and, at the earliest, would be eligible for parole
when she was in her mid-sixties.

Most significantly, the plea avoided the neces-
sity of taking the case to trial. Jury trials were a
risky business. There was always a chance that
someone might believe Arlene's battered wife
tale and she would go free. Arlene Caris was a
very convincing liar, and Bill Ferris was not
about to take that gamble.

Don Delaney was not particularly pleased with
the DA's acceptance of Arlene's plea. If any case
was solid for first-degree premeditation, it was,
he believed, this one. But after years of seeing
how the legal system worked, Delaney had rec-
onciled himself to the plea-bargaining process.
In the Caris case, that would at least result in
Arlene's certain imprisonment. He knew, however, that Belynda Sabloski would have a harder
time rationalizing the plea bargain.

"What do you mean there's not going to be a
trial?" Belynda said when Delaney called her several days before the sentencing. "I thought you
had her on premeditated murder?" Wasn't that
what they had been working toward?

Delaney explained to Belynda the possible out-
come of a jury trial. There was a chance, he said,
that at trial Arlene and Rosalind could pull a fast
one. Between the two of them they could create
enough reasonable doubt in the jury's mind as
to who actually killed Caris. "Your mother could

possibly go free by saying she was covering for Roz," he told her.

"Even though she denies it to me?" Belynda knew she was asking a rhetorical question. When had there been any consistency to her mother's stories?

Belynda believed her mother had indeed shot Bob, but she remained convinced that Rosalind had had a larger role in his murder. Still, she accepted Rosalind's sentence of five years' probation for hindering justice. Roz had, undoubtedly, been manipulated by Mom, had probably been in fear for her own life. Belynda was convinced that Arlene was capable of killing anyone—Roz included—if that meant saving her own neck.

Delaney told Belynda that the minimum sentence Arlene could receive was eight and a third to fifteen years; she would be an old woman by the time she was released.

When Belynda saw her mother walk into the courtroom, she felt a familiar fear but also pity. Arlene appeared utterly calm. She glanced around the room and saw her daughter. Their eyes met, and Arlene smiled. She seems happy to see me, Belynda thought. Her own eyes welled with tears. For however long, her mother was really going to jail.

De Vore's first request was for a delay. His client needed to attend to family matters. The district attorney argued, "I have a funny feeling that other members of the family do not care to communicate with the defendant at this time. If they so choose they could certainly do so at the jail."

Communicate with Arlene? Belynda shook her head. Only days before, Kay told her that some of the family in Georgia wanted Arlene sentenced to death. That had not been an option: the State of New York had banned the death penalty.

Judge Mallon denied De Vore's request for a continuance. The defense next argued for leniency in sentencing. This was, after all, Arlene's first crime. There was no evidence of premeditation "other than unsubstantiated comments by Detective Delaney that there had been prior attempts," and she was hardly a danger to society. Still, De Vore admitted that he was at a loss to explain why Mr. Caris's body had not been disposed of. He told the judge that he had struggled to find an explanation and that it still puzzled him.

Had Mrs. Caris anything to add to her attorney's comments? Mallon asked.

Arlene did. "The only thing I can add to what he said is that I don't have the answers to why. The only thing I know is when this fateful evening happened, when I was hurt, I just lost all cognizance of what was happening. When I did become aware of it, I was scared. I didn't know what to do. I was confused and concerned about my daughter, what was going to become of her and mainly how am I going to deal with this, what am I going to do."

There it is, Belynda thought. The arrogance she had expected of her mother. Arrogance and a stunning lack of remorse. Mom had put a gun to Bob's head when he was asleep, pulled the trigger, hid his body, and tried to get away with it for months, and here she was telling the judge she did it for her younger daughter! Belynda felt pity turn to rage.

"I was just plain and simply scared to death," Arlene continued. "And one thing led into another and another. And I didn't have the answers. Maybe someday I will. But right now I don't have any answers for it, except that I was hurt and lost. It was like something in me snapped, and I was totally unaware. I still cannot tell, even myself, what happened step by step. I think the mental health people have told me that if it were important for me to remember, that perhaps one day I will. Perhaps my intentions were to take my suitcase and walk out of the house and walk away from the argument. That was the only way I knew to stop it immediately. But as well I know, it didn't happen that way.

"Nobody seems to realize that this is my husband that is dead and it isn't that I didn't care for the man. I did. I wouldn't have been with him for over 15 years if I didn't care. I don't have the answers to a lot of questions nor will I ever have. My family is absolutely torn apart. They're at one another's throat. My only reason for asking for a little bit of time is to be with them and try and see if I can reconcile them into dealing with this situation so that I can deal with what I have to deal with."

Mallon: I would have to say that throughout the entire proceedings I did have some concern about, Mrs. Caris . . . that there had been apparently two prior attempts to kill this gentleman.

Arlene: No.

Mallon: Madam, I'm just commenting now from the probation report and also from an investigation from an experienced police officer. It may not be true but he at least came to that conclusion. You are apparently unable now to face up to what happened on that fateful night. I took the plea and I heard your elocution. And from what I can gather from your elocution and also from what you told the probation department, there may have been physical force involved or harassment or verbal abuse in the periods prior to this fateful night. But apparently on this night there was really nothing greatly untoward going on. You cajoled the man into the bedroom and into his bed, and then took the gun and killed him. Now, your protestations of blacking out and not fully recalling what transpired that night, I have to admit, after hearing your own words and reading the probation report I'm not fully convinced that you are not fully able to recall or were not in total control of your emotions and of other faculties that night, and you knew fully well what you were doing, what you intended to do and what you would accomplish by doing it.

Judge Mallon sentenced Arlene Caris to a minimum term of eight and a third years with a maximum term of twenty-five years in jail on the Class D felony: manslaughter in the first degree.
Belynda watched her mother leave the courtroom. Arlene did not look back.

If Belynda had learned anything during her four years of therapy that preceded Bob's murder, it was that running away was one of her biggest problems. She would do just about anything to avoid confrontation. But the foundation on which she had built her life had been so profoundly altered in the year following Bob Caris's death that she knew, for the sake of her own survival, it was time to stop running. She had wanted the truth, had found the truth. She could no longer hide.

So it was with the idea of exorcizing those demons that, in the summer of 1989, Belynda made the two-hour drive from Southampton to Bedford Hills Correctional Facility, where her mother was incarcerated.

The women's prison is situated on the outskirts of the wealthy New York suburb of Bedford Hills, an hour north of Manhattan, off the Saw Mill River Parkway. At that time, Jean Harris was still incarcerated there for killing her lover, diet doctor Herman Tarnower, a crime of passion attributed to the extreme psychological abuse that she had endured. Arlene Caris felt she had much in common with Mrs. Harris. In a 1993 *New York Times* article, Arlene commented on the commutation of Mrs. Harris' sentence after she had served twelve years: "I was glad for Jean. But I was wondering when it is going to be my turn."

Rebecca and Monica wanted to see their grandmother, but they were more curious about the prison. Belynda wanted them to see this was not a glamorous place. This was where women who ran wild ended up.

They drove through a gated entry and parked in a dirt lot surrounded by a fifteen-foot spiked fence. A guard at an outbuilding within the lot told them to place their belongings in a locker; take the key, please. Another guard signed them in: name, address, purpose of visit, any items for the prisoner? Nothing unsealed—that meant no toothpaste, soap, or certain foods within which drugs or small weapons could be concealed. Their palms were stamped with invisible ink. Pass through the gates quickly, please. They went deeper into the prison, through a corridor that opened to a large rectangular visiting room.

It was not so much the noise of gates slamming, of crying toddlers brought by their guardians who waited for sisters and daughters, the mothers of these children; it wasn't even the sad, furtive intimacy between couples. It was more tactile than visual, this sense of despair and humiliation that made Belynda feel naked in a room full of strangers. It was as if she had been stripped of not only her clothes but her skin. There was no protection. She was raw, exposed, dirty.

She told herself she should not have brought her daughters to this terrible place.

When Arlene walked into the room, Belynda immediately noticed the change in her mother. Arlene had put on weight. Her skin was pallid, a grayish tone. She had not kept up her hair; it was white. Mom looked like an old woman.

The rage Belynda nursed driving to Bedford was mitigated by pity.

Arlene gave her grandchildren perfunctory hellos, then settled in a chair. "You better write to Wade," she told Belynda.

"Write to Wade? Whatever for?"

"You better explain to him why you called the police on his mother."

"Excuse me," Belynda said, "but aren't you my mother too?"

"Wade is very upset you called the police. I'm worried what he might do to you when he gets out."

Belynda reminded her mother that Wade was never getting out.

"I don't know about that," Arlene said.

For a few minutes Arlene talked with Monica and Rebecca, about their school, friends. It was extraordinary, Belynda thought, how chameleonlike her mother was. You would think that they were sitting together at her kitchen table; Mom seemed inured to her surroundings. She could become whatever her surroundings demanded, whether that was a trailer park, a country club, or a prison. Did she even know why she was in this place?

Still, Belynda saw that the core of who her mother was had not changed. It was hard, crystallike, immutable in its resiliency and denial.

She decided to ask her about Joel. The question of the urn had bothered her for years. "Mom," Belynda said, "why didn't you pick up Joel's remains?"

Arlene did not skip a beat. "Mr. Brockett was holding Joel ransom," she replied.

Ransom?

"He would not let me take Joel's ashes unless I bought an expensive urn." She did not mention the seven-year-old lie: her supposedly scattering Joel's ashes across the Long Island Sound.

"That's odd, Mom. Because he let me take Joel's ashes away in a box. All I had to do was sign a piece of paper."

Arlene was adamant. Joel had been held for ransom. Yes, for seven years.

Rosalind had visited last week, Arlene told her. She brought Conchetta, her second daughter by Tony, and Danielle. Roz's middle daughter, Christina, the Campanellas' first child, was still in foster care because of a documented history of neglect by Rosalind. Tony was back in jail on assault charges. "I hope she leaves that lazy bum she's married to," Arlene said.

Had Roz said anything about Danielle? Belynda had had custody of the child for only three months following Arlene's arrest. Rosalind had then reclaimed her daughter. "No, but Roz told me you had Christina taken away from her. That was not right. Why don't you have another child if you want one so badly?"

"Rosalind is not fit to be a parent," Belynda said.

"You've always been jealous of your sister."

It was hopeless. Belynda handed some change to Monica and told her to take Becka to the vending machines, buy themselves some soda, cookies, whatever. She watched her daughters standing in line in front of the snack machine alongside children of other inmates. The line of safety between "us" and "them" had vanished overnight. Becka and Monica would always be the granddaughters of Arlene Caris, the woman who killed her husband and put him in the attic.

How could she save them from that stigma? Could she save them from anything at all?

Belynda felt her mother's hand on her knee. She looked into those familiar brown eyes and tried to smile. "What, Mom?" She leaned closer to hear.

"I am going to get even with you and your friend Delaney for putting me here."

Arlene sat back, upright, and smiled as Becka and Monica returned with chocolate chip cookies and soda.

Belynda said they were leaving. Yes, right now. Arlene hugged her granddaughters good-bye. She reached over and took Belynda in her arms. "I *will* get even," she murmured close to Belynda's ear. "I *will*."

In the winter of 1992, Lori Marena, her husband, Henry, and her infant daughter, Kirby, were living in East Quogue, in the Hampton Bays area. She and Henry had been best friends for years. Henry knew her like no other, had been there for her through the worst. They fell in love, and within a day of their engagement Lori learned she was pregnant. She told Henry she would return his ring and have an abortion. She did not want him to feel pressured into marriage. And she did not want their child to feel responsible for forcing a marriage. She would not put any child through that.

Henry told her he wanted the baby. Still Lori waited, to be sure he knew what being a father meant. Six months after their daughter was born, Lori and Henry married. Her father, Fred, walked her down the aisle.

In the years since her grandfather's death the family had fallen apart. Belynda had taken Arlene's threat seriously and moved the family out of state—effectively into hiding. No one but Lori and Kay knew where Belynda, Fred, and Becka lived.

Lori had heard that Tony was back in jail on charges of slitting a man's throat. Doing seven to fifteen, Rosalind had told her blithely on the phone. Roz's five-year parole on charges of hindering justice had been satisfactorily completed. She, Danielle, and the pretty blue-eyed Conchetta had since moved to a squalid trailer court on Old Montauk Highway. Everyone called it Welfare Park. Christina was still at a foster home.

Lori had also heard that Roz's trailer was a pigsty. Pots with moldy food were left in the refrigerator for weeks. Clothes stinking of urine were piled in every corner, waist-high in the bathroom. The girls were often hungry, and the school kept sending them home because of their head lice.

This is what it had all come to, Lori thought one November morning as she drove to work. This was one woman's legacy.

"Grandma would use, use, use you until she drained you of whatever you had to give. She had drained Mom of all her love; Rosalind of all her loyalty; Bob of his life."

On March 28, 1985, when Lori confronted Arlene about lying to her about Joe Marena, she told her, "I will dance on your grave." That was the last day they spoke. Lori told herself, the cycle ends here.

She was stopped at a red light when she spotted Danielle. The girl was waiting for the school bus. Lori had not seen her little cousin in years, but she instantly recognized that sad, distracted expression. At twelve, Danielle was thin, long-legged. She was wearing a short skirt, no stockings, an ill-fitting jacket that could have given her no protection against the frigid day.

Lori wanted desperately to pull over, grab Danielle, and take her back to her own home, where the girl would be warm and safe. But what would I say to her? Lori wondered. Danielle would probably not even know who I am. It's been seven years since we saw each other . . .

> *Aunt Lori, will you bring back my dolly?*
> *Sure, honey. Where is it?*
> *In the room next to where Grandpa's stuffed.*

How to do you make up for all that time?

In Her Own Words: Arlene Caris

[Excerpted from a letter to The Honorable Mario M. Cuomo, Governor of the State of New York, September 2, 1992.]

The Day and Night of the Shooting:

When this tragedy took place, I had not slept

for more than forty hours. I was doing private home health care from eleven p.m. to seven a.m. When I returned home that morning I had already been up for twenty-four hours. As soon as I got into the house, my husband started in on me. He was screaming and shouting at my children again, including my son who had died years ago. Nothing new happened to cause this outburst, just the same old thing again. I was exhausted and tried to get my husband to calm down, but nothing I could do or say stopped him. He continued to follow me around the house screaming and cursing at me for the rest of the day and into the night.

I was so exhausted and I knew I needed to sleep. I tried to go to bed, but he followed me into the bedroom screaming and shouting. This ranting and raving continued through the afternoon and into the night. I kept hoping he would tire himself out and then I could go to sleep. But he continued on into the early hours of the next morning. I thought about just leaving and going to a motel just to get some sleep, but he was so incensed and hysterical that I was afraid he would make good on his threat to burn down the house and my daughter and young granddaughter were sleeping upstairs. I couldn't go up and get them because there was a lock on the door leading up to their room that could be locked from the bottom floor. I was afraid that if I went up there he would follow me and lock us all in. Then if he set that fire he always threatened to, we would all perish.

Finally, I was so exhausted and upset by the hours of harassment that I knew I was at the breaking point. I had to get some rest. I got dressed, packed a bag with the intentions of leaving the house and finding a place to sleep for the night. I was still worried about Rosalind and my granddaughter, but I decided I would leave the house, go to a pay phone and call Rosalind and tell her to get out of the house.

When I was packing my bag, my husband was still cursing and shouting as he laid on our bed. He didn't even notice that I was planning to leave. But when he finally noticed my bag was packed, he went crazy. He slammed me into the bedroom wall and my head hit so hard, I thought I was going to pass out. I tried to get away from him, but he was blocking the exit from the bedroom. I tried going back and forth across the bed thinking I could outmaneuver him and get out of the house into my car. I knew that if I could just get inside my car that I would be safe. He wasn't strong enough to stop a car. He started screaming at me that he knew I was leaving him to go and get a divorce. I told him that I wasn't going to get a divorce, that all I was doing was going to get some sleep and that I would be back the next day. But he wouldn't listen, he flung his wedding band at me and screamed at me that he knew I was leaving him for good. He was crazy.

He kept trying to get at me and I was running around the bed, trying to dodge him and looking for a way out. He struck me on my left leg, sending me plunging headfirst across the front board of the bed. The pain was so bad, I thought my arm was broken. Then I snapped. I don't remember what happened after that. The next thing I remember I was standing by the foot of the bed with my rifle in my right hand. Everything was so quiet and I couldn't understand why I was holding the gun. I had bought the gun when I was living alone with my children years before and there had been a rash of break-ins at the time. I vaguely remember wrapping it up and putting it back in the closet where I always kept it.

The quiet. I remember the absolute quiet. I remembered thinking, at last he's finally asleep, so maybe I don't have to leave anymore. I went into the front room and sat down. I was still so tired, but I couldn't go to sleep. I would just about drift off and then I would stop myself. Something about the quietness kept bothering me. Then I began thinking, why did I have a gun in my hand? I decided to go in and check on my husband. I had a feeling something was wrong. When I went into the bedroom and found my husband covered in blood, I went hysterical. I could not believe he was dead. I am very unclear as to what happened afterwards and what was going through my mind at the time. I know my daughter found me the next morning in a terrible way, confused and bruised. I know she helped me put my husband's body in the attic closet. I can't actually remember doing any of these things, but I know they happened.

I know it was terrible to put him in the attic. A few months before when my husband was in one of his very depressed moods where he was talking about suicide, he talked about how no one would even know he was gone because "no one gave a damn."

I told him this wasn't true because I would know and I would tell his daughter and his brothers. He told me that they didn't give a damn about him and he didn't want them to know he was dead. For that matter, he said, I don't want anyone to know. "Just wrap me up and put me in the attic." I paid no mind to this statement when he made it, but ridiculous as it was, that is what I did after he died. I remember asking myself: Is this what he meant, what he wanted me to do?

The next six months until I was arrested was

a living hell. I worked every hour I possibly could. I was on automatic pilot. I didn't think about anything, I just kept as busy as possible. I told people who asked that he had gone away for a time. I began to believe it myself after a while. If I didn't admit to myself or anyone else that he was dead, then he wasn't dead. I didn't discuss it at all with Rosalind. I refused to accept it. Nightmare is not the word to describe the anguish I went through from then until I was arrested. I didn't know what would happen to Rosalind and her daughter. I was like a robot.

I kept putting in more and more hours at work.

I have thought about that night many times since and I didn't remember anything about it until the day a fellow inmate attacked me with a pen. All of a sudden I had a flashback, where I saw my husband pointing my rifle at me and threatening to kill my daughter, my granddaughter and me. I talked to my therapist about it and he told me that it could have been what actually happened that night or my perception of what was actually happening. Either way, they said, it would be true. Either my husband originally took the gun out and threatened or tried to kill me or I thought that he was seriously going to harm myself and my family and I tried to stop him by taking the gun out myself. I still don't remember what actually happened that night.

Why I Stayed

People have asked me why I stayed with my husband, and I have asked myself the same question since coming to Bedford Hills. If I had left him before that night, this horror might have been prevented. I think I didn't realize that I was being abused. Although my third husband, Robert, was also physically abusive, the main source of abuse was emotional or mental abuse. My first two husbands were primarily physical abusers and their physical abuse had been much worse. If I compared the physical abuse by him to my previous two husbands, it was far less in comparison. What I wasn't able to identify was the emotional abuse that I had endured for fourteen years. Emotional abuse is more horrendous than physical abuse. With emotional abuse there isn't any visible scars or bruises. The scars from emotional abuse are there, but they're invisible and they take much longer to heal. It's difficult to explain, but emotional abuse tears the heart right out of a woman.

I guess I stayed for many reasons. I was ashamed of having made another mistake in my choice of men. I had so much respect for him when I first met him. After my initial disappointment at discovering he wasn't the man I thought he was, I felt sorry for him. I loved him in the beginning and I also felt guilty, he was threatening to kill himself and he really didn't have anyone else. Toward the end, I honestly believed it would get better. I didn't believe it could get any worse. I felt that if I could just stick it out, it would work out in the end. Things could be sorted out if you tried hard enough.

Epilogue

In 1992 Arlene Caris requested commutation of her sentence on the grounds that she had been a battered wife who killed in self-defense; her appeal was denied by Governor Mario Cuomo. On November 16, 1995, her sixty seventh birthday, Arlene Caris was granted parole. She is now living and working on Long Island.

After years in foster care, Christina was returned to her mother, Rosalind, in 1992. Tony is back in prison on assault charges.

In a recent conversation with Investigator Don Delaney, Belynda reiterated her fear of her mother's revenge.

"She's got to have cooled down by now," Delaney told her.

Belynda replied, "You don't understand. My mother never cools down."

She remains in hiding with her husband and her sixteen-year-old daughter, Rebecca.